Is There Not A Cause?

ITNAC

by

Dr. Gary H. Cote

Is There Not A Cause?

Is There Not A Cause? *ITNAC*

By: *Dr. Gary H. Cote*

This book was written in the United States of America.

Published by Kingdom Quest International, Inc.

New Hampshire March, 2017

www.KingdomQuestInternational.com

ISBN 13: 978-1544624181

Is There Not A Cause?

To purchase copies of this Book and More!

To ignite passion for the Kingdom of God!

To learn more about Life in Christ!

To pursue the Love of God!

To know Truth!

To stir Faith!

www.GaryHCote.com

Truth Be Known

Is There Not A Cause?

Is There Not A Cause?

Table of Contents

About The Author

Since 2005 Dr. Cote has been the pastor of a rural church located in Epsom, NH. Amid the irreligious and the indifferent, as well as the indulgent church in New England, the Holy Spirit has been transforming lives, exposing weaknesses, instilling strength, calling for holiness, instructing in His love, and teaching truth. Believers have listened, learned, and lived as the body of Christ; they participate in one another's lives and encourage others to do the same. There are also many others who have resisted or rejected, opting to live their own version of the truth, and stay in their weaknesses. However, those who are saying "Yes" to the Holy Spirit are discovering freedom and the power of His love. They have battled and won, and still battle each day for more. Today, several ministries have been birthed and several ministers of the Gospel have been developed; each serving the Kingdom of God in His grace. They are the fruit that endorses this book and this author's ministry.

Over the years, the Lord has directed Dr. Cote to serve in a variety of ministerial positions and has worked on various tasks. He witnessed numerous situations, and the actions, reactions and responses that left many feeble and spiritually unhealthy. As all of this took place, Dr. Cote looked to God and worked through it all with the Holy Spirit, who guided his thinking and ministry. Dr. Cote purposed in his heart to speak and live the truth, and to put his trust in the Lord (Ps. 4:5). Today, he pastors Merrimack Valley Church, has written several books, and now travels as the Lord's prophetic-teacher to ignite the passion and instruct the people to seek and to serve the Kingdom of God. Amen!

Is There Not A Cause?

About This Book

This book began as a newsletter; it was intended to edify and encourage the church, to inspire and equip believers to live a life in the Spirit, and to stir a desire to battle for all that is good, godly, and glorious in Christ. The newsletter addressed David's interaction with Eliab, Saul, and Goliath as David was stirred by the Holy Spirit to ask the question, "Is There Not A Cause?" This same question has burned in Dr. Cote's heart throughout his ministry. The newsletter became a nine-part series, and Dr. Cote realized it needed to be expanded, therefore, he established it into a book.

Over the years, Dr. Cote observed the various carnality and weaknesses plaguing the church, and the perversions that increasingly pervade society at every level. Many in the church will agree that society needs improvement and revival, but they are unwilling to see themselves in great need of maturity. The church needs sound teaching and a deeper need for admonishment, that is, the church needs a sharp rebuke that awakens believers to embrace the battle, engage in the battle, and to endure to the end. Many call for the sort of revival that moves people to attend church, give tithes, volunteer for ministries, and participate in church programs. However, the revival of the Holy Spirit awakens one to righteousness and moves them to battle. This book was birthed with that objective.

As you learn from this biblical text, I hope and pray that your interest will be sparked and you will in turn ignite faith in others. In addition, it is important for the church to begin

Is There Not A Cause?

asking David's question and be moved to action. Action proves the genuineness of your faith. The true biblical message is never focused on "feeling good," nor does it seek to make someone "happy" or to ensure that you feel good about yourself. Therefore, this book centers on maturity, to equip believers for ministry, and to battle for the joy, peace, and righteousness that is found only in the Holy Spirit. This book is to stir faith, while instructing, correcting, warning, and calling all to live a life of truth, humility, and righteousness as wholly devoted followers of Jesus Christ.

Is There Not A Cause?

PREFACE

Eight hundred years before King Saul began to reign over Israel, the Lord told childless Abraham that his descendants would inherit the land of Canaan; thus the area was called the Land of Promise. According to this promise, the Lord called out to Moses to deliver the Hebrews from Egypt and established the Covenant of Law. Then Joshua was appointed by the Lord to bring them into the land and established the people as a nation. Though possessing the land, it was during the Times of the Judges that their inner heart was revealed. During that four-hundred year period, the Bible records that everyone did what was right in their own eyes, as there was no king in Israel (Judges 17:6 21:26). They did evil.

Their evil hearts wanted wicked ways and their loyalties always went to other nations. They only cried out to God when the oppression became too great and every other method of deliverance failed them. They cried out for a king, but they wanted a king like the other nations; one who would fight their battles for them. They were weak and fearful. Their motive for a king was self-centered. Israel rejected the leadership and authority of the Lord God; they despised the goodness of His character and His righteous ways. They loved the other nations, their ways, and their false gods.

The prophet Samuel would be the last Judge and the prophet who would usher in the Times of the Kings. He would anoint King Saul as well as King David. In so doing, the Lord set two forms of leadership and servanthood before the people of God and before all believers. King Saul would

Is There Not A Cause?

be more concerned with serving himself and would prove to be self-righteous in all his ways. Though he was anointed to be king of Israel, Saul opted to honor "self" whenever opportunity presented itself. His insecurities and sense of inferiority always won his loyalties; his need to be praised, followed, reputed, and regarded overrode every decision. Saul was not sound in his ways. Though he was the anointed, he rejected the cause of the anointing in order to serve his needs.

However, David was also anointed by Samuel, but unlike Saul, his anointing proved to be glorious because he lived a life that said "Yes" to the Lord, even when he failed or faltered. David faithfully served God because he had a heart for God. He was righteous and proved fit to rule. He trusted in the Lord and placed his faith in God's Spirit. David's anointing reflected the Holy Spirit's presence and power. David's life and leadership demonstrated the cause of the Lord; his anointing was fixed to a heart of faithfulness.

David was a young man who was prepared and proven faithful in the furnace of monotony and insignificance. His humble heart and deep trust for the Lord God unfolded in the oven of harsh treatment from others, especially from King Saul. Refined in these fires, his godly life would show forth the righteous man who loved the Lord. When those with calloused hearts mistreated him and misspoke of him, rather than carry offense or seek personal retribution, David turned to the Lord and cried out to Him. When others looked to make themselves look grand by attacking him, David always relied on the mercy of God. In so doing, David wrote numerous

Is There Not A Cause?

psalms, expressing his heart for God and his full trust in Him. Through David's life, God's character, conduct, and concerns became known; through his various experiences and multiple encounters, every believer can also know the life of faith that pleases God and this life certainly involves David's question, "Is There Not A Cause?"

Is There Not A Cause?

Is There Not A Cause?

INTRODUCTION

The twenty-first century is saturated with deception and delusions, decadence and depression, defiance and doubts. Simply, disobedience abounds in every sphere of life. Unrest is present everywhere, because unrest is in the heart of the unbelieving person. Therefore, chaotic lives result as anxiety plagues the heart and stress envelopes the mind. Sadly, this same condition has entered the church. Christians are not living a life of victory and freedom; rather, a host of excuses have been employed to side-step issues, avoid pain, and fill the void. Christians are seeking various pleasures and amusement, whether music, movies, games, crafts, or sports, all trying to bring some excitement to life. So many simply want to cope through each day; Sunday's Service has become a means to feel connected, feel saved, and praise the Lord in order to gain a spiritual escape, but, there is more to life!

This is the result of unbelief, which now saturates the heart of numerous Christians, who now presumptuously think they are believers because they agree with the doctrine. Unbelief is deeply influencing the church. Many Christians have become lukewarm in their faith. They no longer arise to fight the good fight of faith, rather, most are content to get through-the-day or to just simply, "get-by." Often you will hear the reply, "hanging-in-there," from both the worldly and the believer. This just should not be the case.

In addition, please consider this current-day problem; that is, many Christians are using current-day evils as a benchmark to measure their superior standards and to gauge

13

their own idea of rightness. There is very little passion for the Kingdom of God, as many seek out numerous ways to enjoy the "self-life," and then they go to church on Sunday to "praise the Lord," hoping to feel better about themselves and life in general. They agree with the return of Christ, but do not reflect on the weight of this truth or the dire warnings given regarding His return that will establish His eternal Kingdom. Others will acknowledge Christ on a regular basis and will sing songs of praise and dance in the aisle, but they will not surrender to His cause. They are content to passively coast through each day, struggle with its problems, and complain as they find someone to listen. They avoid living for Christ fully and completely, thinking that it will just add more difficulty to an already stressful life. A host of pastors and preachers have given themselves to the ministry of helping you "feel saved," rather than "live saved." This is not victory!

However, surely there are still those who desire truth in the inward parts as David wrote (Ps. 51:6). There are still those who understand that God rules in truth and His cause is worth the fight. The prophet Elijah discovered this as well; amid complete idolatry, immorality, injustice, and indifference, the Lord told Elijah that there were still seven-thousand who had not bowed a knee to the false gods (1 Kings 19:18). This same prophet will be the Lord's witness prior to His return in glory.

There is a cause worth standing for, and it is time to act with the same intensity and desire of David, who was stirred by the Holy Spirit. The quest of this book is in alignment with the heart of God, as demonstrated through David about three-

Is There Not A Cause?

thousand years ago, that is, to fight the good fight and ask the same question: "Is There Not A Cause?" (1 Sam. 17:29). May this book ignite your faith and instruct the people of God in their pursuit of God's Eternal Kingdom.

The people of God must begin seeing everything and everyone with God's perspective; they must be seekers of His righteousness, and pursue His love and holiness. The people of God need the inspiring presence of the Holy Spirit. Those believers are passionately interested in seeking the Lord, speaking of His Kingdom, and willingly and faithfully serve Him wholeheartedly. They will set their minds on things above, see the world's evils, and know God's answer. The quest is to bring forth a revival of consecration; it is the "ITNAC" movement, that is, "Is There Not A Cause."

David asked this question so many years ago and it must stir in your heart as well. David boldly asked, "Is there not a cause?" David's older brother mocked him, yet David asked the question. Then David's faith intensified and his question caused commotion in the ranks until he met face-to-face with King Saul. Even though Saul contended with him and confronted him with the thought of inadequacy, David's heart pursued the question until he was face-to-face with the menacing problem, Goliath. Faith accepts the fight.

This question, "Is There Not A Cause?" must resound in the heart of every believer. As you read this book and consider the biblical text that records David's battle with Goliath, may you discover the biblical mandate to engage in the battle which was presented by the Holy Spirit to every

15

Is There Not A Cause?

believer. David's burning question is rooted in the Spirit, and recorded by the Spirit. The question remains, preserved for over three-thousand years for each believer to ignite their faith to embrace the battle, engage in the battle, and be willing to endure the battle till the end. Right now, it is simply time to begin. Right now, this is the time each believer must ask the same question, "Is There Not A Cause?"

The faithful will always be interested in advancing the Kingdom in their lives and in others. The battle is real. Yet many fear the unknown or they do not want to disrupt their comfort zone; many do not want to deal with their own inadequacies, insecurities, or inhibitions. Many have a resolve in their heart on Sunday morning, but end up letting the difficulties, monotony, and drudgery of Monday Morning to win them back to passivity and uselessness. Their timidity toward the battle has won so often that they do not know how to walk and live in the boldness of God.

A revived heart must first be awakened to its own sinfulness. Then, it must be moved to brokenness as you realize your great need for the Savior. Here, you discover the depth of His power to face the enemy and walk away in victory. Weakness will cry out for attention, but you must learn to rely on the strength of the Holy Spirit. The useful anointing will be rooted in a heart that is after God's own heart; the useful anointing pursues the character of God, seeking to do His will, His way, according to His word. David was this man! Hence he asked, *"Is There Not a Cause?"*

USEFUL ANOINTING

"But the LORD said to Samuel,
"Do not look at his appearance or at his physical
stature, because I have refused him. For the LORD
does not see as man sees; for man looks at the
outward appearance, but the LORD looks at the
heart" (1 Samuel 16:7).

Is There Not A Cause?

Every person's life is a reflection of their belief system toward God. What you truly believe surfaces in everyday life; therefore, every person is displaying their true value system. A person worships whatever or whoever they value, and they do so to the extent of importance. The greater value placed on some relationship, person, or thing, will dictate every thought and action in daily life. The greater worth receives the deeper regard. There is a present fear of losing it; therefore, a person will take steps to ensure its security.

King Saul gave little regard to God's purposes or plans, and thought little of his role in the Kingdom of God. When Saul was anointed to be king of Israel, he was searching for his father's few donkeys and could not find them. He was not aware that they were missing and he could not find them, and he did not care greatly. Seeking the answer from God was the last resort and was only at the urging of his servant. Saul's reluctance to seek the Lord was the core of his being. The anointing to be king would not change his self-centered ways. Though he was given a new heart when anointed by Samuel to be king, nevertheless, his desires for personal respect and regard always overrode his passion to seek the Lord.

In contrast, David grew up as a shepherd. He was the youngest of eight sons; therefore, he was given the seemingly unimportant task of watching over his father's sheep. Later on

18

Is There Not A Cause?

the eldest brother would hint that Jesse's flock was basically small in number. This would indicate that Jesse was not a wealthy man, nor his family. David's life was spent alone in the fields, a place of testing for him.

David lived his days under the stars, the moon, and the sun. As a shepherd, he would have endured the cold and the heat, the rain, frost, and the snow. Jacob knew this life well, and described the shepherd's role and responsibility when he confronted Laban. Jacob said:

> These twenty years I have been with you; your ewes and your female goats have not miscarried their young, and I have not eaten the rams of your flock. That which was torn by beasts I did not bring to you; I bore the loss of it. You required it from my hand, whether stolen by day or stolen by night. There I was! In the day the drought consumed me, and the frost by night, and my sleep departed from my eyes (Gen. 31:38–40).

This was David's life; he was a shepherd, a difficult life and one without honor. The Egyptians despised the position of a shepherd as lowly and unbecoming (Gen. 46:34).

The seasonal elements created enough issues for most to cause complaint about their lives, but David humbly served. Besides the environmental hazards, David dealt with the beasts that preyed on the flock, and David was the sole barrier between the devouring beasts and the flock. David engaged in battle to save the sheep from the predator's slaughter.

Also, David had to contend with the despair that often accompanies loneliness and the monotony of life. This combination leads many people to illicit sin, indifference, and

Is There Not A Cause?

bad decisions; it also usually results in actions and reactions based solely on impulse, while robbing their soul of all joy and peace. Despair, depression, despondency, or the downcast heart is found within the realm of monotony and loneliness. This combination ruins many lives, monotony affects the need to be important, while loneliness plays on the desire to be accepted, approved, and affirmed by others. Saul was plagued with despair, as things did not go as he planned, thus causing problems for himself. Problems are simply that—things not going the way you want them to or expect them to go. Many become frustrated, aggravated, irritated, or agitated, and then lash out, withdraw within themselves, or seek a way to relieve the self-imposed pressure. This is called, Stress!

Many try to manage their stress and say that there is too much on their plate. This is the foolishness of the self-life that does not place trust the Holy Spirit. Stress is an aspect of the natural man; the Holy Spirit is never stressed or in a state of distress. Jesus never worried. A person's emergency never became His urgency and a person's urgency never became His emergency. Stress and distress are the weakness of natural man; everyone deals with it, but the believer looks to the Holy Spirit, cries out to Him, and then casts all burdens unto Christ.

While in the field David conducted his affairs rightly and carried out his tasks faithfully. He did not seek great things for himself, which is a major cause of stress for many people. David simply lived his life under the canopy of God's provision. He was under the watchful care of the Holy Spirit, though he lacked full understanding and was unaware of

Is There Not A Cause?

God's plan for his life. Nevertheless, he trusted God. While caring for the sheep, the Holy Spirit was actually preparing him to be the king of Israel. In the field and in this environment, the Holy Spirit was forming this unknown boy's heart to shepherd the people of God.

Assigned to watch his father's sheep, David was unaware of God's plan for him; to shepherd the nation and the sheep of God's pasture. The Holy Spirit will use many tools, situations, circumstances, and a variety of people to fashion your heart rightly. The Holy Spirit will dig into your soul to root out any sense of self-importance and self-centeredness. If any is left in the heart, it will surface, especially in times of offense. When David was praised by the women, who honored him above Saul, envy rose in Saul's heart. He wanted the greater praise; self-importance plagued him. This envy brought ruin to Saul and his actions caused suffering for many others in the nation; all because he had the need to be honored and regarded above all others. Unlike David, Saul sought great things for himself. This is still the plague that ruins many and robs their future.

You will find it difficult to deal with anyone who is still afflicted with the self-centered life; they will be argumentative, combative, and easily provoked when anything is deemed out of place for them. They are easily offended and will carry that offence to justify their ego. Sometimes they will first employ flattery or politeness, and appear nice and helpful, but if things do not go as desired, the self-centered person's spirit will take over and battle for supremacy. Whenever a person is concerned mainly about his

Is There Not A Cause?

or her own sense of well-being and the need to satisfy their own needs, then you have someone who cannot be trusted.

King Saul had the need to be recognized, reputed, and rewarded; he wanted the credit; he wanted to be seen and known. Simply, he was the king, therefore, he expected all others to honor him accordingly. This need was never dealt with in the core of his being; therefore, it constantly flared up and controlled his decisions.

In contrast, David was a young man who fought for his father's sheep, battling the paw of the lion and bear; while King Saul did not know where his father's donkeys were and could not find them. The smallest task inconvenienced him and befuddled him to exasperation. Saul was like that donkey.

The little things in your life matter, and they reveal the big things to those who have ears to hear and eyes to see. Many Christian parents dismiss the small things; they do not want to fuss with all those little things. They do not realize that the spirit world operates in the sphere of the seemingly insignificant. The "rolling of the eyes" is a clear message; the way a child cleans up or takes out the trash will reveal much. Parents must watch for the insecurities, inferiorities, and inadequacies that hound a young person's soul. If left unchecked, coping mechanisms will be employed by the child as they grow; they will learn to apply what works for them, and these coping mechanisms are never healthy, never helpful, and will lead a person to cope rather than conquer. Unfortunately, many parents and teachers, as well as numerous pastors, preachers, and ministers have never learned

Is There Not A Cause?

this for themselves, therefore, they miss it altogether or do not have the spiritual understanding or skills to confront it. The church is currently plagued with such lack that it is causing many to be feeble in their faith. You must consider the small things in your own life before you can be entrusted with more. As Jesus said:

> He who is faithful in what is least is faithful also in much; and he who is unjust in what is least is unjust also in much. Therefore if you have not been faithful in the unrighteous mammon, who will commit to your trust the true riches? And if you have not been faithful in what is another man's, who will give you what is your own? ... And he said to him, "Well done, good servant; because you were faithful in a very little, have authority over ten cities" (Luke 16:10–12, 17).

The Holy Spirit was present and active in David's life long before the day he was anointed by Samuel to be king. In the day-to-day grind, you will find the Holy Spirit at work in your life. The little things reveal the big things, and in the little things you will hear His voice teaching you to humble yourself, obey the faith, trust the Lord, flee from sin, and forgive those who spitefully offend you. Sadly, many believers today do not care to know the manner in which the Holy Spirit prepares people for life in Christ. They are too stressed out with life's issues; this keeps them hardhearted, blind, and deaf to Him. They never walk rightly before their God, humbly seeking Him in all things. They are troubled with life.

Is There Not A Cause?

David was a young man of about seventeen when the prophet Samuel entered his city by the direction of the Lord. Samuel arrived in order to anoint God's elected king. Samuel passed over each one of Jesse's sons, yet the Lord rejected each one, though the first surely looked the part. He was tall and seemed to fit kingly status, just as Saul pleased the people when they saw him standing a head taller than all other men. Samuel thought the eldest son, Eliab, was the Lord's king, but the Lord rejected him. The Lord's word came to Samuel and instructed him and every believer. He said, "Do not look at his appearance or at the height of his stature, because I have refused him. For the Lord does not see as man sees, for man looks at the outward appearance, but the Lord looks at the heart" (1 Sam. 16:7).

The Lord's eye was on another; therefore He bypassed the seven older brothers. Saul's height gave him great favor among the people and Samuel was led to think in like manner, but the Lord made clear that His election was beyond the flesh. All seven sons were refused, till there seemed to be no more. Rather than Samuel questioning God, he questioned Jesse. With no sons left and knowing that the house of Jesse was chosen, Samuel then asked the question: "Are all the young men here?" (1 Sam. 16:11). David was ignored and even slighted; he was not deemed worthy to be invited. Whether he was considered too young or just insignificant by the family, the Lord ensured that His plan and purpose would be known and established. David was the Lord's choice.

Is There Not A Cause?

You never have to secure a place or position for yourself. Learn to be content with the task set before you, and do all as unto the Lord God, and not for the eyes of man. Learn to please the one that sees with truth; learn to live for the majority vote of the one, true, living God. Living to please man and gain their approval, attention, or affirmation will lead you to stress and frustration. You will begin to manipulate and maneuver in order to gain and achieve your desired objectives. Many may applaud your success, but the applause will fall short as it did for King Saul. The sons of Korah wrote, "For men will praise you when you do well for yourself" (Ps. 48:18). Being a man-pleaser will always leave you empty, whether trying to please a parent, child, friend, or foe. The true believer seeks to please God; faith pleases God.

The Spirit of God uses everything, everyone, and every experience or event to prepare you for His work in the kingdom. For David that meant watching over his father's sheep; a task that was passed to him as each of his brothers would have also experienced. But for God's man, it was not a burden unto drudgery, but a blessing of deliverance. This small job was common for young boys, but the Holy Spirit's work is never common. In the midst of your preparation, trust God for all things and be thankful in all things as well. Remember, David did not know he would be king, the writer of Psalms, and the recipient of an eternal covenant that would bring forth the Christ.

David's eldest brother, Eliab, was bypassed, as were the other brothers, then David was revealed and anointed to be the

Is There Not A Cause?

king of Israel. He was chosen to replace Saul in due season, according to the Lord's timing. Surely Eliab's ire was aroused and envy stirred in him. This ill-will would surface later. David would come from his father's house and enter the business of the Kingdom of God, doing his Father's will, that is, to shepherd a nation and illustrate for all believers the value of God's anointing presence.

In the process of time, the armies of Israel were once again at the battlefield contending with the antagonistic Philistines. Jesse wanted David to bring supplies to Eliab and his brothers. However, it was the timing of the Holy Spirit to bring David to this hour; the time when he would arise and be known as a warrior. David set out to complete Jesses' directive, but he was actually setting out to accomplish the Lord's plan and purpose. David was about to be known to Israel, to the nations, and to every believer till the coming of Christ and throughout God's eternal kingdom. David's one step brought him into his future; he was more than an errand boy; he was the servant of the Lord Most High.

When David arrived on the battlefield, he was ready for so much more. He was made ready to meet the enemy and do battle because his trust in the Lord surpassed any fear, hesitation, apprehension, or self-concern. David already had experience facing fear, timidity, insecurity, and apprehension. The Holy Spirit already brought the lion and the bear into his life in order to face the weaknesses of the heart; he learned to trust and it prepared him for his future. Hence, David clearly saw the predicament of the Israelites. He understood!

Is There Not A Cause?

You are not ready to know others until you rightly know yourself, and you cannot know yourself or see yourself clearly, until you have met God face-to-face. Then, He will undertake the task to show you your weaknesses and teach you to rely on His strength. David was taught to trust in the Lord's strength. The power of David's anointing was rooted in his obedience to the faith. David sought to please the Lord. The will of David was the Lord's will; he did not continually try to get his will to do God's will; rather, the Lord's will was David's will. The desires of David's heart were not satisfied by the Lord; rather, David's heart was satisfied by the desires of the Lord. So many in this day preach and teach that the Lord's powerful presence is to fulfill your desires, as though the Holy Spirit honors the desires of the flesh nature in some way. Rather, you must realize and accept that the Holy Spirit gives you His heart, mind, and purpose; His desires will be rooted in you and flourish accordingly. Never think that the anointing of God is to satisfy or fulfill self in anyway; this experiment was tested and proven false through the life of King Saul. The useful anointing is the anointing that is in harmony with the plans, purposes, and promises of the Holy Spirit. The apostle Paul said, "Only do not use liberty as an opportunity for the flesh" (Gal. 5:13). The apostle Peter wrote, "Yet not using liberty as a cloak for vice" (1 Pet. 2:16). These anointed men of God knew the purpose of the anointing and their heart's desire reflected it. Saul failed as he chose his own way, thus forsaking the Lord. Learn from them!

27

Is There Not A Cause?

The Danger of Allowing Insecurity in Your Life

About twenty years ago I was listening to a Billy Graham crusade. Billy invited a man to tell his story about losing his son to drugs and how to this day he asked the question of himself, "Why did my son take his life?" and "Why did he take drugs?" In his story, he referenced the boy that he once walked to school and then casually said with a chuckle, till the day when my son stopped me on the sidewalk as we walked and asked me to go no further with him. The father asked the boy, "Why?" The boy replied that he did not want the kids at school to see him being walked to school by his father. Dear readers, this is the little thing that revealed the big thing. This is the story that helped me see more clearly. The boy was already making decisions to be a man-pleaser, which led him to coping mechanisms in order to find acceptance. The boy chose to give the greater regard to his friends at school than to his own father who loved him. This little thing was the time to instill boldness and secure his identity in Christ, but insecurity won. The father shrugged it off and smiled, but the son was lost to the cancerous presence of insecurity.

The Appearance of Succeeding

General George Patton of WW II was known for his toughness; he relished in presenting an ominous figure of himself. He would practice his stance and his appearance while looking in the mirror. He was presenting a persona. Why, because he was actually insecure about his high-pitched voice. General Patton tried to make up for his perceived lack. General Patton was hiding his insecurity behind a veil of a tough exterior. If the General would have ever turned to the Lord, the Holy Spirit would have immediately started to work on the inner core of his being and called to face this weakness and surrender it, and that word was not in the General's vocabulary. Patton was the General, a leader, and facing his sense of inferiority or inadequacy was beyond his desire.

Is There Not A Cause?

Facing The Family
David And His Brother, Eliab

David was a young man of about seventeen years of age when he was anointed to be king over all Israel. Though young in age, he was already full of faith; his trust was tested and found to be in the Lord God. When he came to the army of Israel, who was encamped on a hillside overlooking the Valley of Elah, he saw the Philistine army across the divide facing and opposing Israel and, therefore, the Lord God as well. David also saw the situation more clearly than anyone else; he was seeing with the Lord's eye. Faith sees spiritually.

David heard the voice of Goliath rise up from the valley floor unto the mountaintop where the army of Israel stood; though they had the high ground, none dared move forward. Goliath's voice was one of defiance and a complete disregard for Israel and for God. The men saw him and were dreadfully afraid and dismayed. All perceived confidence and thoughts of victory and bravery had left their heart. However, David's faith was stirred.

David was rightly irked and his ire was raised because of Goliath's taunt, but mostly he saw Israel's dismayed presence. They had no will to face Goliath; they mainly spoke of what the king would do to reward anyone who would kill Goliath. Insecurity will focus elsewhere, rather than face the fear.

Hence, Eliab directed his own frustrations and lack toward his young brother David; the one chosen instead of him.

Is There Not A Cause?

Eliab's own anger was directed toward his young brother, instead of Goliath. Eliab spurned David and then he proceeded to mock him. Eliab revealed his own heart when he jabbed David saying, "I know your pride and the insolence of your heart, for you have come down to see the battle" (1 Sa. 17:28). David did see the armies aligned, but there certainly was no battle between the armies; the battle was one of fear, insecurity, unbelief, and boasting. The battle was spiritual. David witnessed Goliath's insolent attitude toward God and Israel, but it was heightened when Eliab's fear surfaced and sought to bring David into question. When David turned to address Eliab's rebuke he asked the question that should burn in every believer; he said, "Is There Not A Cause?"

The young David was chosen by Samuel to be king. The prophet passed by Eliab, who was older, taller, and initially preferred by Samuel; now Eliab was most irritated by David's question. Eliab revealed his own insecurities and his pride attacked David, trying to soothe his own shortcomings and appear strong, brave, and capable. Eliab's faith failed. Though tall in stature, he was short in faith.

Stress and tension will always result when the man of faith arrives and begins to confront the natural-mindset. Faith and fear will clash, expect it to be so. As your faith deepens, know that battles will surface. When a person of faith is present, friction will result and it produces a heated relationship in some way. David's presence irritated Eliab; he saw himself worthy to be king, yet the Lord saw the desire in Eliab's heart.

Is There Not A Cause?

Eliab had no courage to confront Goliath, therefore, he attacked his younger, smaller brother; this is weakness trying to look strong, brave, and righteous. Beware of such weak people; they abound and saturate the church. They are easily offended and will try to look spiritual in some way. They want people to see them as godly, loving, good, or holy, depending on their needs. If they are in some sort of leadership position, they will love the titles and relish in the attention. Usually they will lead in one of two ways, either by consensus, seeking to please others, or with a calloused heart, not actually caring about others, such as Saul.

Eliab was taller than David and the firstborn, whom Samuel eyed as the sure thing, but Eliab was of the natural mindset. He was refused. God was looking at the heart of the man. The naturally-minded man can be professionally trained and deemed ready for battle; he can make the proper assessments and arrive to the conclusion that makes sense to every other man; but the man of faith will see the answer to the problem that supersedes the natural-minded man's conclusion. When Eliab saw himself set in comparison to Goliath, then he saw himself unable, just as the Israelites thought when they saw the sons of Anak, the giants of the land who occupied areas in the Land of Canaan.

David saw Goliath with God's eyes and his faith was stirred to believe God for victory. The anointing on David moved him to action. The Holy Spirit's anointing presence always stirs one's faith to action; He is never a sedentary presence. Eliab compared himself to David and attacked,

Is There Not A Cause?

because when he compared himself to Goliath, he fell short. Those of the natural mind will compare themselves to others and to the problem, rather than looking to the promise of God and relying on His presence and power for victory.

Today's ministerial boasts are based on being the tallest midget in the room and the healthiest patient in the hospital. This may sound prejudicial to you, but you must see the picture clearly. Denominational ministries and ministers climb the ranks and have learned to look caring and spiritual. Many determine success by the flatteries of others. They say that it is never about the numbers, yet their conversations are always centered on the numbers. Boasting about being the tallest among the shortest is not wise; to boast that you are more healthy than the others does not make you whole nor healthy.

You may learn what to do and be told what to do, but in times of pressure, then the anointed man surfaces. The anointed person is moved by faith and faith moves the anointed person to action; it goes beyond and deeper than academia, where many today talk about faith. David was moved by faith that conquers.

Eliab, Saul, and Goliath were all known for their height, but one's physical stature does not equate to faith, power, anointing, godliness, or approval. David did not consider his height as an obstacle, whether as a strength or as a weakness; his mind was on God. Whatever you see as your strength and weakness will be the comparison you use to judge others. Anointed faith acts on the cause of Christ and will leave comparisons to God. Faith values the anointing.

Is There Not A Cause?

David knew God's position and posture toward unbelief, unrighteousness, and ungodliness. Therefore, he never gave regard to Eliab's unrighteous jabs, to Saul's question of unbelief, or to Goliath's ungodly taunts. As David would write years later: "Blessed is that man who makes the Lord his trust, and does not respect the proud, nor such as turn aside to lies" (Psalm 40:4).

David could have yielded to Eliab's overbearing presence. The eldest of eight sons meant that there was a good deal of age between them. Eliab was much taller and knew how to thrust himself forth and assert his presence. Based on David's reply to Eliab, it reveals that this was not the first occurrence like this. David said to Eliab, "What have I done now?" This rhetorical question needed no response; the revelation of his relationship with Eliab was housed within the question. Eliab's highmindedness was exercised on David.

If David cowered or attempted to explain in order to win his brother's approval, then David's faith in the Lord was small. David's first challenge or battle as the anointed king came from his own family. Everyone who wants to mature in the Lord will have to face family, friends, and the familiar. The believer sees and determines things by the mind of Christ. Therefore, a believer will be confronted by those of the natural mind within their own families. God arranged it to be so; by this the people of faith are made known; they are willing to choose the ways of the Lord God in place of familial acceptance. David won. David always turned to God.

Is There Not A Cause?

So many Christians are giving place to various faces of pride, unbelief, and a host of lies and delusions in their life, in order to avoid a difficult situation or person, especially in their own families. Beware of giving favor to anyone who is ungodly, unrighteous, or in a state of unbelief; it will invoke God's disfavor, rather than His good pleasure. Faith will speak, stand, and step is accordance and in alignment with God's plan and purpose. David demonstrated the proper response when he faced Eliab, Saul, and then Goliath.

David was not deterred by his brother's scorn. Family dynamics did not rob David of his faith. He continued to ask the question going from one to the other asking the same thing, "Is There Not A Cause?" The Spirit of God was on David's tongue and his persistence stirred the crowd of soldiers who stood on the sidelines in battle array. These soldiers of Saul were on the hillside ready for battle in their attire, but their hearts were weak, frail, feeble, and most timid. Each day they dressed for battle and arranged themselves in order, yet each day they looked upon the enemy who simply taunted them and their God with an undeniable mocking spirit. They were dressed for battle and looked battle-ready, but there was no heart for battle. Timidity was in their heart, but David's cry of faith was stirring them.

David's question moved the soldiers to listen and each one replied in like manner; they heard his question but responded by telling him about the reward from King Saul if he could kill Goliath (1 Sam. 17:27, 30). They focused on the benefits, not the cause. David's question went from one to the next

Is There Not A Cause?

until his ongoing quest to be heard was finally heard; the people told Saul, who summoned David to his presence.

Beware, Christians today are doing the same thing as Israel; they are sitting on the sidelines praying for help and hoping for deliverance, which often times reflects more wishing than praying. They want the enemy to simply go away so they can get back to their own lives and concerns. Many believers will be willing to dress for war, but they are too fearful to engage in battle. They look at the enemy's presence and hear the mocking tongues rise from the valley where their crops grow and the water flows. All that the Lord God gave them is occupied by the enemy, yet no one is making a move. They eat and drink in the comfort and safety of the camp, and watch the enemy each day mock them. Yet no one is confronting the enemy that devours souls, steals their provisions, reviles their God, and occupies their land. Christians seem willing to reside on the hillside and talk about the terrible times and the ferocious enemy in their land.

Today's Christian does not ask David's question. Why? Because they do not want anyone stirring their own hidden fears; they wish it would all just go away. They fear losing their present comforts. Convenience ungirds every decision. They do not want their daily life disrupted. Sadly, many do not arise because it assaults their own sense of dignity and pride. They possess a superficial trust in the Lord that gets exposed if they step out in faith. Each time the enemy jeers at them, they get aggravated and wish God would do something about it.

Is There Not A Cause?

I have often witnessed believers call upon God to take a stand against the devils for them, yet they fail to submit to God and resist the devil, as James instructed (James 4:7). They pray for God to deliver them or someone else, and to fight for them; however, they will not do the same thing on this side of the battle. They simply cower. They do not fight for the Lord, yet they pray, "Whatever it takes Lord, do it." These believers can be strong, battle ready Christians on Sunday morning, who rebuke devils, plead the blood, pray out loud, sing songs of victory, and call upon God, yet go quiet through the week. Many will encourage one another with various flatteries saying, "You're a good person" and "At least you're trying." They give their tithe, read their Bible, and take notes during the sermon, yet at the next hour they are at the restaurant or store being careful to offend no one with prayer. They are hyper-sensitive to any look of disdain and will consider this as suffering for the Lord. Once home, they are ready for relaxation and will tread lightly around the so-called "unsaved loved ones," fearing they would lose their beloveds if they take a stand for the Lord in their own homes. Really? Is this the trust that wins souls? Where is the victorious trust?

Today's believers are all about discussing the battle and the war; books are written, preachers address it, and we tell each other about trusting in the armor of God. However, all is done within the camp set up on the hillside, standing and sitting on the sidelines, ready to flee the scene if the enemy charged. Many have the armor of God in their mouth and

Is There Not A Cause?

encourage one another to put their armor on before they go out into the world, but their daily activity reflects little of a battle scene. For them, life in the Spirit is all about getting through the day and surviving another day. They try to be happy with their lives, but they have willfully or ignorantly forgotten John's statement of truth, "You are of God, little children, and have overcome them, because He who is in you is greater than he who is in the world" (1 John 4:4)?

Believers must start asking the same question that David did so many years ago, to be stirred in order to stir others. We must listen and look for others who are of like-spirit and of like precious faith. The apostle Peter wrote to the church and addressed the church this way: "Simon Peter, a bondservant and apostle of Jesus Christ, to those who have obtained like precious faith with us by the righteousness of our God and Savior Jesus Christ" (2 Pet. 1:1). There are others who have been stirred or want to be stirred for the cause of Christ. There are believers who truly want the Lord God's concerns to take precedence over all others. These are the ones who will seek to answer the call, "Is There Not A Cause?"

The victory that David would gain over this beast of a man began with a simple question, "Is There Not A Cause?" Though rebuked by his own family, he persisted; he opted to give greater regard to God. This led to a stirred crowd; his faith was ignited and his confession of faith moved others to consider the cause. The Holy Spirit's question was David's confession and it landed David in the king's presence, now seeing Saul face-to-face. Now what?

Is There Not A Cause?

The prophet Micah said, "Do not trust in a friend; do not put your confidence in a companion; guard the doors of your mouth from her who lies in your bosom. For son dishonors father, daughter rises against her mother, daughter-in-law against her mother-in-law; a man's enemies are the men of his own household" (Micah 7:5–6).

The man named Job discovered this truth when his own wife said to him, "Curse God and die" (Job 2:9). Joseph discovered the envy and wrath of his brothers as did Moses when he was confronted by Aaron and Miriam.

Jesus said, "Whoever denies Me before men, him I will also deny before My Father who is in heaven. Do not think that I came to bring peace on earth. I did not come to bring peace but a sword. For I have come to 'set a man against his father, a daughter against her mother, and a daughter-in-law against her mother-in-law'; and 'a man's enemies will be those of his own household.' He who loves father or mother more than Me is not worthy of Me. And he who loves son or daughter more than Me is not worthy of Me. And he who does not take his cross and follow after Me is not worthy of Me."

Jesus emphasized serving God wholly and faithfully saying, "If anyone comes to Me and does not hate his father and mother, wife and children, brothers and sisters, yes, and his own life also, he cannot be My disciple" (Luke 14:26).

Then one said to Him, "Look, Your mother and Your brothers are standing outside, seeking to speak with You. But He answered and said to the one who told Him, "Who is My mother and who are My brothers? And He stretched out His hand toward His disciples and said, "Here are My mother and My brothers! For whoever does the will of My Father in heaven is My brother and sister and mother" (Matt. 12:46–50).

USEFUL AUTHORITY

"The LORD, who delivered me from the paw of the lion and from the paw of the bear, He will deliver me from the hand of the Philistine"

(1 Samuel 17:48)

Is There Not A Cause?

Facing Authority
David And King Saul

One of the greatest tests in the believer's life will be in the sphere of authority. In this realm, humility is forged and proven, and loyalties, faithfulness, and obedience are known. Flourishing in the Lord has often been sidetracked because a person did not know how to rightly relate with authority. Think on Saul who usurped the word of the Lord with his own and did not complete the Lord's command against the Amalekites. Instead, he opted for his own way. He then excused himself before the Lord's prophet as though all was well. His core desire was to gain the praise of the people; he said to Samuel, "I have sinned, for I have transgressed the commandment of the LORD and your words, because I feared the people and obeyed their voice (1 Sam. 15:24). Saul's lack in regards to authority cost him his appointed position. His authority was useless.

Since Satan rebelled against the Lord God, then authority will always be part of the equation. The very term "Kingdom" implies the presence of authority and the need to submit. However, there is only one useful authority, and it is not found in a title or in position, but soundly in your relationship with the Holy Spirit. Therefore, unbelief always negates it.

David's question was burning in the ears of everyone present. The spirit realm was also stirred as this young man began exercising the authority of the Lord God. The armies of

Is There Not A Cause?

Israel were under the command of King Saul, but useful authority was housed in the heart of a young man named David, a shepherd who knew the cause and character of God.

David was brought to stand in front of King Saul. He was in the king's presence because he had that burning question residing in his heart, "Is There Not A Cause?" This simple question was rooted in the Holy Spirit. Regardless of the response or the lack of response from the armies of Israel, David pressed the question. This question was from the Holy Spirit. David was not deterred by the mocking, the rejection, the accusations, or the lack of enthusiasm. If David would have quit speaking, then he would have simply faded away in the day. But the question would have remained in the heart of God, because the question is calling for action, and that question must become your quest. Surely there is a cause.

Everything was escalating and David's question landed him squarely in Saul's presence; David was meeting the king face-to-face and they saw each other eye-to-eye (1 Sam. 17:29–31). This was the first of many encounters to come. Of course, the Holy Spirit made all the arrangements. King Saul's replacement was a mere shepherd boy, a young man with a heart for God, who was courageous and determined.

When David met Saul, Scripture records that David was the first to speak, and his statement exposed the true problem and revealed the remedy; he said, "Let no man's heart fail because of him (*Goliath*); your servant will go and fight with this Philistine" (1 Sam. 17:32). Any courage that might have been in the king's heart or in his army was quenched upon

Is There Not A Cause?

seeing Goliath's presence and hearing him bellow from the valley below. The king and the armies of Israel feared Goliath; he left them paralyzed from any action. One man's greatness eliminated their entire pool of glory. One man's ferocity quenched Israel's faith. The people of God, the army of the Lord, were diminished and drained of all confidence, thus exposing their lack of faith and trust; they were in dread of Goliath. But David's bold statement revealed the answer to the problem as well; by one man's faith, the ungodly presence of Goliath shall be swept aside. David will go and fight!

A tremendous utterance of boldness! David entered the king's presence and gave no place for Saul to speak. He spoke faith immediately by the Spirit. Picture David before King Saul speaking of their fear and then follow it up with the faith for victory. So many make such bold statements today, yet they do not follow it up with any act of faith that supports it. For every bold statement, there must be a bold step that matches it or else it was merely pretense. Without a step, this is just a brazen statement; just someone looking to be considered spiritual. So many are in church today speaking a bold faith, while keeping their eyes on the reactions and responses of others in order to evaluate their affect and satisfy the needs of their insecurities. Christians often talk about praying for others, but quiver when it comes time to pray for someone outside of their comfort zone, that is, the manner in which they like to be seen by others. They have surrounded themselves with those who relish in their spirituality. They do not rely on Christ's great power; they simply talk of it to

Is There Not A Cause?

others they already know believe the same way. They rest in the orderly ranks of the army of the Lord. They do nothing in fear of someone's taunt, scoff, or glance of disapproval, especially among the respected family members like Eliab. They fear accountability, so they do not act on a thought that comes from the question, "Is There Not a Cause?"

David's remedy meant he was now accountable to it; he was not a fake looking for place among them. Even more so, his statement also said that he would be victorious; not that he would just try, nor that he was simply willing, leaving some element of skepticism in play in case it did not work out. He declared victory over the giant. The step had to bring victory, not just step before Goliath and call it victory. David had to go into that valley, engage the enemy, and bring victory.

Faith sees the victory and acts accordingly. Faith sees past the problem and always sees the problem-solver at work. David's willingness was not youthful exuberance with an unfounded faith. David was not a man of pretense. David was not operating from a desire to be seen and known by man, if so, he would have immediately defended himself when his older brother jibed him at the battle line. This was not pride at work, though his brother saw it that way. Pride in a person will often times see another's boldness as boasting, because this arrogant spirit filters their own thoughts and perverts the proper perspective of anything godly. David saw victory because he knew God and he knew victory. David was not disrespecting the king; rather, he was honoring God.

Is There Not A Cause?

Many can enter the safe confines of the king's tent and make bold predictions and statements full of faith, only to falter like cowards or fail like any other when it comes time to put a step to it. Somehow the bold faith uttered in the tent lost its place when it came time to step out in front of the army and before the enemy. Nothing ever gets accomplished, nor is any victory won simply because someone was spewing bold faith. Any weak, spineless individual can do this. There must be a step of faith before any victory is accomplished.

The victory that is gained in a Sunday Morning service must show up when your feet hit the floor on Monday morning. There should be a continued walk of faith into Tuesday as well and through the week. Victory is available in all things, regardless of the circumstances or situations developing; the believer must know the Holy Spirit is present, active, and advancing the Kingdom of God. Whether you are washing floors, cars, windows, or laundry; whether you are a salesperson, corporate professional, or bricklayer; the Holy Spirit calls you to believe Him and trust Him for victory.

"Is There Not A Cause" was the question. The problem was fear in the heart of every individual suited up with armor who could not find the courage to step out and believe God. The problem was a heart of timidity, which feels taunted by anything that is not in alignment with its shameful insecurity. The problem was a king who could not see past his own inferiority. The answer came from the one unlikely to achieve anything great for Israel; the remedy was resting in the heart

Is There Not A Cause?

of one young man who believed that this challenge was God's battle and he was ready to step out in faith.

Why do so many Christians fear stepping out and engaging the enemy? Simply, they give greater value to their own lives; they prefer their places of safety. They want "me-time" and seek to enjoy the "me-life." They do not want their comforts and conveniences disturbed; therefore, they let the Lord do His own fighting. Their inner thought says, "Beware, count the cost before you step out," as they consider the potential loss to their own comforts and conveniences. The cause of God is never the foundation to their thinking and planning; rather, it is their own lives. They are willing to dress in the armor, come to the battlefield, talk strategy, gather along the battle lines, and submit to the king's authority, but they do not exercise God's authority and step out to fight the good fight of faith. They will flatter themselves with the thought that they are willing; they will soothe themselves with the spiritual command to be in submission to the king, but their allegiance is covering their own fears. The scriptural truth that reveals, "The battle is the Lord's" is no longer our reliance or fuel to step forward in the fight; rather it has become our excuse to do nothing.

Many applaud those who stepped up and out in time past, and thank the Lord that He raised someone up to do so, but they will not take their own stand, not even with their own friends and family members. They cry out and say, "We need revival," but they want God to raise someone up, just not them. Why not? They fear the jeering army and taunts from those close to them. For many, they soothe themselves with thoughts of battling Goliath and tell themselves that they would fight for God if the Lord empowered them or called them to do so, yet they do not take any step to do so. Useful authority begins with a heart to believe God and a willingness to step out, even in the smallest of ways. Great battles are won by the unknown foot soldiers who obeyed their commander's orders. "Is There Not A Cause?" *Be BOLD In Christ!*

Is There Not A Cause?

Facing Unbelief
David And King Saul

As a believer you will face unbelief. The most dangerous form of unbelief comes from those who acknowledge the truth and agree with the tenants of faith, but fall short when it comes to applying it in life. Unbelief will be a constant battle in your own soul, but you must come to the place where you believe God instead of give place to your own fears. You will face unbelief in fellow believers who may mean well, but work against the very victory that gains freedom. You will face unbelief in leadership, whether a pastor, teacher, or parent. King Saul's unbelief kept an entire army paralyzed. A parent's unbelief can keep an entire family feeble and full of insecurity, even though they attend church, sing the songs, give an offering, and read their Bibles. But when it comes time to fight the forces that oppress, they shy away, thus preferring their own fears. Should someone attempt to confront this lack, then they are willing to contend with the very one trying to help, but they will not fight the true oppressor or face their own unbelief.

While David stood and contended with King Saul, the burning question was still in his heart: "Is there not a cause?" David said to the king, "Let no man's heart fail because of him (*Goliath*); your servant will go and fight with this Philistine" (1 Sam. 17:32). As this statement came to Saul's ears, something else was stirring in his heart; it was the

Is There Not A Cause?

familiar unbelief that plagued his forefathers and still influences so many today. He said to David, "You are not able to go against this Philistine to fight with him; for you are but a youth, and he is a man of war from his youth" (1 Sam. 17:33). Saul's first response exposed his heart; he walked by sight in all things and not by faith. Saul immediately compared David to Goliath through the natural eyes. Saul only saw the size of the young man, not the size of his faith. He actually saw his own sense of smallness in Goliath's awesome presence. Goliath's taunts found their place in Saul's heart; he was highly affected by the fearful stance that Goliath took before Saul's entire army. There was no courage in Saul's heart; his spirit was drained. As Samuel said to him earlier, "When you were little in your own eyes, were you not head of the tribes of Israel? And did not the LORD anoint you king over Israel? (1 Sam. 15:17). Those insecurities were rooted in his unbelief. The same is true for you; unbelief always robs you of courage and strips you of any ability to lead or live rightly. Saul was transferring his fears to David; he did not receive them.

Beware of such activity in your life, that is, those who soothe themselves by justifying their own fears to you and often attempt to support their thinking by gaining your agreement. In so doing, they rob you of any will to believe God. If you take on the mantle of unbelief, you will walk away with your head down, that is, downcast. You will feel defeated because unbelief was cast upon you and you gave it regard. You gave a nod of approval, thus giving it power in your soul. A person may express his unbelief with a polite and

48

Is There Not A Cause?

caring voice, or a prayerful and sincere concern, but unbelief is unbelief, regardless of the attire it uses to cloak itself.

The unbelief that settled in Saul's heart was the same unbelief that was housed in the heart of the Israelites even though they were delivered from Egypt. Moses sent twelve spies into Canaan in order to spy out the land and report their findings; ten gave a bad report saturated with unbelief. Though the land was profitable, they saw everything through the natural eyes of unbelief. They saw that there were giant men living in the land and said to Moses and to all the people, "We are not able to go up against the people, for they are stronger than we...The land through which we have gone as spies is a land that devours its inhabitants, and all the people whom we saw in it are men of great stature. There we saw the giants...and we were like grasshoppers in our own sight, and so we were in their sight" (Num. 13:31–33). The people put their trust in a report that was absent of faith. They looked passed the Lord God's presence, promise, or purpose for them; they did not consider the Red Sea rescue or the wilderness miracles. No authority could move them beyond this point. They were stuck in the quagmire of unbelief.

Failure follows those who discern and decide in a state of unbelief. Useful authority must stem forth from a heart that believes God and makes the Lord their trust. As David would write, "Blessed is the man who makes the Lord his trust, and does not respect the proud, nor such as turn aside to lies" (Psalm 40:4).

Is There Not A Cause?

Today we see many teaching, preaching, and writing about leadership and trust; many college courses are centered on leadership issues, often focusing on ways to manage people and deal with conflict resolution. However, true leaders are men of faith who step out and believe God as David was so inclined. Numerous church leaders have bought into the modern notion that leaders are determined by those who are following them. This foolishness says, "If no one is following you, then you are simply taking a walk," as John Maxwell has written. Many propagate this idea and think they are wise.

Disregard such humanistic thinking. This is useless authority and carries no value in the Spirit; it is void of the faith that steps forth and forward at the leading of the Lord.

David did not wait for a following before exhibiting leadership. When he tried to muster the troops on the hillside, no one followed him. They listened to the rant of a youngster, but no one said, "Let's Go." David simply turned away from one and turned to another and said the same thing. The Spirit of the Lord came upon David when he was anointed by Samuel and the Spirit of the Lord was speaking.

When he finally came to Saul's presence, he entered the tent alone. No one went with him. When he arrived, Saul's voice of discouragement was waiting for him. Now what? Shall he go through a "let's try to convince them all" program? Shall he design and develop a consensus? Shall he have meetings and try to explain to everyone how it is going to work, tell them about faith and trusting God? No, he simply said "I will go," and he had the full faith to do just that.

Is There Not A Cause?

David was a leader who followed God; this is a true leader. Whether people followed him or not, David followed after God. His heart sought the Lord. His eyes were on God's plan and purposes; he did not look around or turn aside to see who was alongside him; nor did he turn his head back around to see who was supporting or following him. He did not ask for a vote of confidence as many do today in ministry. David's eyes were on the Lord and he stepped out ready for battle. Anyone who keeps turning around to see who is following is surely an insecure person and will certainly falter. This leader is not being led by the Spirit.

Saul was this sort of man; he needed a following in order to be deemed a leader in his own mind. The anointing did not fulfill him, nor did he find the power to command from the anointing. One of the first things he did as king was to choose three thousand choice men, those of high-caliber, to follow him wherever he went; this decision gave his insecure heart a false sense of confidence. However, his confidence was easily shaken. Saul's system to cope with his insecurity fell short anytime he perceived the loss of praise from the people; then he would react in an attempt to regain his following.

Earlier, when Saul faced the Philistines in battle, he noticed the people becoming nervous as they waited for Samuel to arrive; then they started to leave the battlefield. Saul's unbelief prompted worry and stress; therefore, he became impulsive. The action of the people determined Saul's reaction. Saul did not possess the authority that stemmed forth from the anointing; he relied on his own thinking. Saul was

Is There Not A Cause?

rebuked by the prophet Samuel for foolishly offering the sacrifice unto the Lord, which was quite presumptuous and beyond the scope of a king's duty. Yet, Saul was concerned with one thing; he said to Samuel, "When I saw that the people were scattered from me, and that you did not come within the days appointed, and that the Philistines gathered together at Michmash, then I said, 'The Philistines will now come down on me at Gilgal, and I have not made supplication to the Lord.' Therefore I felt compelled, and offered a burnt offering" (1 Sam. 13:12–13). His fear was not overcome by faith, rather he succumbed to his fears, seeing everything from the natural and he assumed destruction would come upon him. He did not make the Lord his trust.

Saul also showed his continued disregard for the Lord's command through his blatant disobedience and rebellion with the Amalekites. Samuel confronted Saul once again and Saul immediately tried to talk his way out of the confrontation. Saul said, "I have sinned, for I have transgressed the commandment of the Lord and your words, because I feared the people and obeyed their voice" (1 Sam. 15:24). Saul knew his core problem and out of his own mouth confessed the issue. Saul always gave greater place to the words of man, instead of the word of the Lord. Saul was not a man of faith.

Saul feigned repentance by confessing that he sinned, but his repentance fell short of changing his ways. His heart's desires were centered on himself. Samuel pronounced the Lord's judgment on Saul. Though rejected, Saul was mainly concerned with one thing and it was not repentance or

Is There Not A Cause?

surrender to the authority of God. Rather, he sought to secure his leadership amid the face of the people and said to Samuel: "I have sinned, yet honor me now, please, before the elders of my people and before Israel, and return with me, that I may worship the Lord your God" (1 Sam. 15:30).

King Saul was established as king by the Lord God, yet he referred to the Lord as, "your God" and the people as "my people." Saul's confidence to lead was found in gaining acceptance by the people, instead of the anointing of the Lord God. He just wanted to be seen as noble and display himself as spiritual in the eyes of the people. Saul's self-life always surfaced and tainted his authority. This need for praise and acceptance would eventually come forth in full force when David gained the favor of the people; when the women sang and danced after David's victories, "Saul has slain his thousands, and David his ten thousands" (1 Sam. 18:7). This infuriated Saul and would move him to fiercely attack David.

King Saul displayed the heart that can never be the Lord's warrior that is ready for battle. Saul's inner fears made him fully afraid of Goliath's presence and power; he saw himself as small and in a diminished capacity. However, David saw the situation with God's own heart. He compared Goliath to God's almighty power and presence; therefore he uttered, "The Lord, who delivered me from the paw of the lion and the paw of the bear, He will deliver me from the hand of this Philistine" (1 Sam. 17:37).

David's comparison was one of faith. He took authority over the situation. Faith would ask, "What is this beast of man

Is There Not A Cause?

who dares to mock God Almighty?" "What sort of man can stand before God who displayed such contempt?" Goliath took the very breath God gave to him at birth and used it for his own glory. This giant warrior was only sustained by the breath God gave him, yet he held nothing but scorn for his own Maker. His body drew breath from the pools of God's provision, and then exhaled with a voice of defiance. Such raw ungodliness was presented before the armies of the Lord and only David saw it rightly saying, "Who is this uncircumcised Philistine, that he should defy the armies of the living God (1 Sam. 17:26). For forty days Israel had been kept stagnant and most paralyzed by one man who displayed tremendous arrogance, who was trained in warfare since he was a youth. This man was an idolater who worshiped a false god named Dagon; this devil was surely gloating in the spirit realm as Goliath asserted himself before God's cowering people. However, once David showed up, things changed.

David had already experienced the Lord's favor when he dwelled in the wilderness and fields with his father's sheep. There, he learned to battle the beasts and came to understand that the battle is the Lord's. He also knew that victory cannot be gained unless someone steps out and believes God. The sheep did not save themselves from the devouring, menacing beasts. The Lord did not send an angel to rescue the sheep so that David would be undisturbed, secure, and happy. The bear and the lion would have had their way unless David had stepped into the gap and changed the course of events. The Lord could easily have kept David safe and the sheep secure

Is There Not A Cause?

without any adversity. However, faith would not have been forged or made known. By grace you are saved, through faith.

David knew he could slay Goliath because of his previous experiences; the Lord gave him victory to protect the sheep. David's boldness was in his confidant trust that God was with him. David learned to trust the Lord, to call upon Him, and to know His ways. You cannot gain victory over Goliath if you flee the threat of the lion and the bear. Victorious living is a learned development; it is a step-by-step progression. You must gain victory in the smaller things in order to acquire victory in the Valley of Elah; the place where two forces are in opposition, and the fate of either is determined by faith and fear. Consider your current battles and choose faith that sees and says as the Lord sees and says. Is There Not A Cause?

Too many believe in the existence of God, but very few simply, "BELIEVE GOD." Many Christians agree with the biblical doctrines, yet walk a life in defeat and a sense of hopelessness. There is victory in faith. David witnessed success in battling predators and knew God was with him. He looked to those experiences. David was anointed by Samuel, bypassing his seven older brothers. Surely now the Lord was not leaving him in the valley to die at the hands of this giant. In like manner, Christ died on the cross for you; the Holy Spirit has come and now dwells in you, and the promise has come forth that He will raise you from the dead. He has made you His witness. Therefore, "Let God arise, let His enemies be scattered, let those also who hate Him flee before Him" (Psalm 68:1). The Holy Spirit has not brought you to new life

Is There Not A Cause?

in order to cast you away. Simply believe God for every victory and build a series of steps that are victorious.

Every believer must trust the Lord with all their heart; it is never satisfactory to just state belief in God. Merely believing in God can be accomplished by anyone, even demons believe in the one, true God and they tremble at this truth (James 2:19). Churches are saturated with a belief system that is in agreement with the doctrine of belief, but very few are willing to step out in alignment with that faith. David believed God! Can any believer sit idly? Does rest mean idleness and passivity? The Lord promised peace and joy in the Holy Spirit, but does this mean "vacation"? Useful authority leads you to victory, but the useful anointing is the power.

Today, too many just want to make friends with the bears and the lions, domesticate them, train them, and feed them. Many of the modern-day ministers have become circus trainers as they work to keep everybody at bay and in order. They call this ministry. They want to hug the devourer and win over his favor, but a bear and a lion are beastly and are never anything more. Even parenting has taken on the role of circus-trainer, as parents struggle to keep everyone happy. This is not the life of victory in Christ and it certainly is not the useful authority that comes by having the Holy Spirit in you. The anointing of the Holy Spirit will move you to exercise proper authority in the battlefield of your own home.

Goliath was a beast and David saw him correctly. Often times Christians will equate Goliath to the devil, who antagonizes and assaults the people of God. Surely he does

Is There Not A Cause?

so! However, Goliath characterizes the flesh nature. Goliath epitomizes the overbearing presence of the flesh nature. There is only one answer. The Goliath nature must be done away with in every believer's life, giving the flesh nature no regard. Doing so cuts off the devil's influences and sets you on the path of chasing down the enemy. David knew that Goliath must be slain, not won over with politeness and niceties.

In today's church culture, many are turned-off by this sort of teaching and preaching. They opt to develop their own way of winning, which never works; it just makes them feel righteous and loving. Any Christian, who rejects David's lesson plan or attempts to sidestep this teaching in some way, will surely end up being feeble. Any believer who draws back from this lesson plan will be unfit for battle; they have entered the realm of unbelief. If any Christian ignores the battle, then he or she is untrustworthy, hence, one who cannot be trusted. Faith makes a man of God ready for war. A man of war is ready to complete the campaign.

Is There Not A Cause?

Facing Motives
David And King Saul

David stood before the King of Israel. He was not there to gain favor for himself, nor was he trying to make a place for himself. Though there was a reward available to anyone who would challenge and defeat the beastly Goliath, David's eye was attentive to something greater and his ear was honed to hear God's deeper call. His faith in the Lord heard the voice of the Spirit, while men in battle array stood looking over the valley and remained deaf to the call of God. Their eyes only saw Goliath, while David's eye saw the uncircumcised Philistine for what he really was, a mere man bellowing forth boasts that were fueled by devils.

David heard of the reward when he arrived on the hillside, but that was not his motivation to act. Saul promised great favor to any person who could defeat Goliath; he also promised a royal position in the family through marriage with his own daughter, and he offered a life free of taxes for the victor's family (1 Sam. 17:25). David asked about the reward, but was not motivated by it. His elder brother scorned David for asking the question and giving attention to it, but David would not be set aside by man's pride that seeks to excuse its own weaknesses by making another feel small. Rather, David asked, "Is there not a cause?" David's faith was riled.

Men of war were on the hillside standing shoulder-to-shoulder, but they had no zeal and no courage to engage in

Is There Not A Cause?

battle. Why? There was no faith or trust that victory could be gained, but there was the fear of losing their life and the fear of failure. Unsurety is cancerous. Many were enticed by the reward, since they talked about it on the hillside, but the reward did not move them to action. The reward got David's attention, but not because of its value, but that such value was not moving anyone to action. Evidently there was a great need present to warrant such a reward from the king, yet the king could not move himself or anyone else in all Israel to engage in battle. Saul placed his hope in another. For forty days Saul was in the tent wondering what to do about Goliath.

Beware of being motivated by this sort of earthly prize. Gehazi had eyes for the things of this world and he got Naaman's leprosy with it. Achan envied the valuables of Jericho and suffered the same fate that fell upon Jericho. Eyes must not be set on the gain and glory that is among the ranks of men. Beware of those who look for ways to advance themselves among their peers and seek an audience with those in charge. There is an ever-present, growing trend to gain position, pay, and place among ourselves; they are "climbers" and "opportunists." Men often applaud each other when someone moves upward among them; they will be surrounded with those who are likeminded. Their success is determined by titles and they will enjoy the applause of men; more so, they will consider that praise as deserved and even a blessing from the Lord. However, in this sort of increase there will be very little anointing, as men and women simply flatter each other. Their authority is in the title and position granted to them by other men, and they will often rely on various rules and various forms of legislation to achieve their ends.

True faith has a disdain for such things; faith is fueled with a love for God that is equaled with a disdain for sin. Sadly, many believers operate in the realm of self-promotion, seeking advancement among the elite. David would one day be honored as the king and he will receive the title fully knowing it was of the Lord. David's quest to face Goliath was not an idea in order to advance himself to the throne. The Holy Spirit was making all the arrangements; David was the surrendered vessel. Therefore, a day will come to bring the Ark of the Covenant to Mt. Zion and he will dance before the Lord, giving no place to the dignity of self that plagued Saul.

Though David asked about the rewards, he was not moved by them. He was motivated by Goliath's assault that spewed words of contempt for God and His people. David was not looking for a following; he was concerned about who he was following. We need the faith that will get stirred in the same manner that riled David.

Too often, today's believer is set to prove himself as a polite and nice person, and quickly defends his integrity and loving heart should anyone challenge his love. Many have become so soft and weak in their resolve, and so calloused toward the Spirit's presence and purposes. They want to be seen by men as a caring Christian, instead of a godly man full of faith, ready to battle those in opposition to the life and love of the Lord. David's ire was raised and he sought action. David was not being presumptuous; he was filled with

Is There Not A Cause?

righteous indignation. He did not look to usurp Saul's authority at any time; he was submissive to him at all times, but he spoke and walked faith.

David's quest for victory was stirred by his question, "Is There Not A Cause?" He was now in the presence of King Saul and he was there to do the Lord's bidding. He answered to man only as it fit the Lord's plan and purpose. David told Saul, "Your servant has killed both lion and bear; and this uncircumcised Philistine will be like one of them, seeing he has defied the armies of the living God" (1 Sam. 17:36). David referenced himself as Saul's servant, though David himself was anointed to be king. David served Saul as he served Jesse, faithfully. This must be the heart of the believer who desires to serve God. The heart of Saul was full of fear, and all those under his leadership were quivering in their armor. David served as unto the Lord; he knew the Lord's presence, power, and purpose. David would confront this problem called Goliath, but he could not conquer Saul's lack of faith, his insecurities, or fulfill his need for attention. There are battles to be won, but you cannot conquer another person's heart or manage them into freedom. They must overcome for themselves. You set the pattern. Many cause themselves undo harm because they work hard trying to get someone to believe and do right. You can teach it, preach it, and write about it; you can encourage and set the pattern worthy to follow. But you cannot conquer the heart of anyone who is unwilling to surrender, submit, and serve God. A person can only serve to the extent that he or she was willing to submit, and a person can only submit to the depth of his or her surrender. Saul never surrendered; he just lived as king.

Saul just wanted the problem to go away, as so many do today. Today's Christian will often pray with one central focus, that is, "Lord, make my problem go away so I can be happy and healthy." Many are frustrated because God has not made some particular problem go away. This is unbelief at work in them. In every situation, circumstance, and relationship, the Holy Spirit is at work.

Saul was the appointed royalty, but that did not mean that anointed royalty was present. David, however, possessed God's cause in his heart, thus superseding any fear that may be present. Faith must always be greater than one's fears, trusting in the cause of God. David's heart was being quickened by the Lord, rather than quaking at the situation. The psalms reveal that David had many fears come upon him, but he always knew where to bring his burden. The presence of fear surfaces in life, but the answer is to trust in the Holy Spirit fully and completely. Faith overcomes every fear. The apostle Paul wrote to the church in Corinth and said, "We were troubled on every side. Outside were conflicts, inside were fears" (2 Cor. 7:5). Yet Paul was motivated and impassioned with a faith and a love that superseded his troubles and fears. The believer must be motivated by truth, love, faith, and hope, knowing that God is faithful. When you believe, you will trust in God's authority, and you will operate in God's authority. This is useful authority and it leads to the true armor of God.

USEFUL ARMOR

"And Saul said to David,
'Go, and the LORD be with you!' "

(1 Samuel 17:37).

Is There Not A Cause?

Facing The Fight

Armor For War

When Saul saw that David was determined to go forth into the valley of Elah to face Goliath, he consented to it and said, "Go, and the Lord be with you" (1 Sam. 17:37). Saul was willing to put his faith in David, but he was not able to put his faith in God directly. He heard David's words, but could not hear the commands of God in David's word. Saul could declare blessing upon David, but could not walk in that same blessing. Saul hoped that the Lord would go with David, but excused himself from going with David. Such leadership abounds with many, but faith never acts this way. David was determined; the Spirit of God makes you a person of resolve. The blessing upon David was not rooted in Saul's faith; rather, Saul confirmed the truthfulness of the matter.

Saul was a head taller than all his countrymen; this aspect of his physicality won the favor of Israel when they saw him as their new king. However, when Saul faced someone taller than himself, his faith was arrested. His desire for the battle stopped short if the cost was deemed personal. David was shorter in stature, but possessed a tall faith and a deep faith. The measure of a man is never according to the natural, whether by the physical or by the applause of man.

Saul yielded to David's request and he then gave David his very own armor, since David had none. A shepherd boy in the field had no armor of his own; David only had experiences of

Is There Not A Cause?

God's presence as he defended his father's few sheep in the midst of a field that was flanked by the marauding beasts of the earth. David protected these sheep from both lion and bear, and this Goliath of man was nothing more than a beast, attempting to snatch the sheep of God from the pasture. He would defeat this beast as well. David's armor was useful armor against such devilish beasts.

Saul's own armor rested quietly on the side, and he proceeded to put it on David (1 Sam. 17:38). Saul surrounded himself with three-thousand choice soldiers, yet still could not bring himself to put on the armor that stared at him each day.

Saul had his own armor put on the young shepherd. David's body was covered by Saul's coat of mail and the bronze helmet was put on his head. David then fastened Saul's sword to the armor and tried to walk; he failed miserably. How humorous this actually must have looked, watching David walk in armor that was made for someone taller than all other men of Israel. The armor was not for him; it was not the right fit; it could not be trusted. He could not move in it at all; it suffocated his freedom; it was awkward.

David took off the useless armor. There is an armor that is made by the hands of man that never protects a person rightly in battle. There is an armor made for show and there is an armor made to war against men, but useful armor is found in the faith. This was David's armor; one that was tried, tested, and found to be true. David's trust in the Lord aligned himself with the character, conduct, and concerns of God. This is the armor that results in victory. This is the faith that can stand fast in the face of terror and step forward against evil.

Saul saw that David was ready for battle in his heart and he released him to fight; but he had to add his own plan to the process by putting his own useless armor on David. The very armor he refused to put on his own body and use against Goliath, he put on David. If the armor did not provide courage to Saul, who owned it, how could it encourage David? If Saul's faith was not in that armor, then how could David trust it? This is not the way to battle. The armor that brought no courage to Saul was certainly not going to be the Lord's method of defeating Goliath. This was useless armor; it made David awkward, not free. The armor stole away his faith and caused him to trust in another person's advice and opinion.

There will always be those who want to clothe you in their way of doing things. The flesh nature will always seek to insert itself in some way to share in the glory of someone's success. Should David win the victory, Saul could say that it was because of his armor. If David succeeds, all would see him clothed in the king's armor. However, if David failed, Saul could also run to the thought that he warned him beforehand, telling him that he was but a youth facing a man skilled in war since he was a youth. Flesh inserts itself whenever there is some glory to be gained, but leaves a way out for another to suffer the shame. Always consider where a person is at in his or her own life before you accept their advice, guidance, help, opinion, or support. As the Bible says, "Remember those who rule over you, who have spoken the

Is There Not A Cause?

word of God to you, whose faith follow, considering the outcome of *their* conduct" (Heb. 13:7). Consider the results of their family and ministry, the words they use, the jokes they laugh at, and the things they post. Weigh the things they look forward to in life, that is, their objectives. Ask: what does their ministry look like? What sort of person follows them, listens to them, and why do they do so? What does their faith look like when adversity or trouble comes? What offends them and how do they handle offence? When they find failure in their midst, how do they handle it? Are they often sullen?

Now consider the devil's ploy to offer you confidence for your fear, whether it is a timidity or insecurity issue. The devil also has an armor to protect your inner fears and insecurities from being seen or known. He cloaks you with arrogance and stirs your ego; pride is the devil's answer to your fears. Insecurity will hide itself behind the spirit of pride. However, pride always plays you as the fool, but keeps you blind from its affects. When you are cloaked in pride, then you never see rightly. Pride will twist the truth and will assault anyone or any opinion that might expose your inner weakness. Beware! Pride is saturating the church; many operate by opinion, judge things by feelings, and are so easily offended.

Humility is always the answer; humility aligns rightly with the Spirit of God; humility gives no place to the devil's influences since it does not seek great things for self. Humility places all of its attention on the Holy Spirit. Humility simply trusts in the Lord and does not seek place for self, nor does it try to defend itself or justify itself if assaulted with a faulty

Is There Not A Cause?

accusation of wrong-doing. Humility is not concerned with hiding its own inadequacies, inferiorities, or insecurities; rather humility openly confesses weakness and then places full trust in the Holy Spirit. Humility looks to the character of God, rather than seek to justify its own character. Conversely, humility does not seek to be known and reputed; it leaves such things in the hands of the Holy Spirit.

Useful armor is armor that is not of this world. The armor of God does not bring courage, rather, it is courage. Useful armor does not simply offer you protection; rather, it prepares you for war in heavenly places, against principalities and powers of the air. These evil spirits influence nations and individuals to war with each other, and advance all forms of wickedness in every culture. Useful armor is from the Holy Spirit's presence and it seeks to diminish and destroy the words of contempt that war against God. Useful armor battles against the thoughts that seek to undermine truth and the wisdom that ascends from the minds of devils. The apostle Paul said, "For the weapons of our warfare *are* not carnal but mighty in God for pulling down strongholds, casting down arguments and every high thing that exalts itself against the knowledge of God, bringing every thought into captivity to the obedience of Christ" (2 Cor. 10:4–5).

Useful armor is for battle, not decoration. An armor that is so easily set aside while the enemy taunts is not an armor to trust in. A person may have advice and offer ways to help you, but be aware that many are merely playing "dress-up" when it comes to fighting in the faith. An armor that makes

Is There Not A Cause?

you look like a warrior on the battle line, but does not move you to advance in the valley, is not useful armor. There are those who say that they are ready to do great exploits for God, but facing Goliath is usually not one of them. Most have not overcome the paw of the lion and the bear. If a person has not overcome his own flesh nature, be careful when listening to his guidance or trusting in his help. Saul was planning and ruling through the flesh nature, and this nature is never in alignment with the divine nature.

Consider your life in the Lord right now and ask the Holy Spirit to pinpoint the armor you trust in. Where do you turn for support? What fears overcome your soul? Are those fears rooted in the loss of things in the natural realm? Do you have a support system that feels like useful armor, but it is truly not found in the Lord? Would your armor fit in David's story?

Saul's useless armor permeates our society; it comes in the form of self-help books, various pills and medicinal hope, and in counseling sessions to give you a place to talk through your offenses, hurts, and feelings. However, all of them are useless and awkward when facing the real threat. Goliath is present, fuming threats of defiance, and ready to war. Goliath assumes that he is unbeatable. Goliath must be dealt with in order to gain victory over demons, and this Goliath is the one looking back at you in the mirror each day. Many do not want to contend with their own defiant and decadent nature. The apostle Paul said to the church in Ephesus, "And (you) were by nature children of wrath" (Eph. 2:3).

Is There Not A Cause?

In our modern-day church world, there is an enormous rise of those who talk and teach on the armor of God. The armor of God is referenced and encouraged, yet so many are so willing to set the armor of God aside just like Saul did when faced with a great battle. When the battle they fear rises in front of them, they go to prayer and call upon God to help them with this great trial, but they refuse to engage in the battle themselves. They just want someone to deliver them from the problem. Useful armor is ready because the heart has been prepared for battle by the Holy Spirit. Armor is not merely for survival, but it is for advancing against the enemy.

The Saul-type leadership or ministry wants victory so they can do as they have always done before. There will usually be great discussions about the situation, deep theology may surface, and battle plans are considered, but most are unwilling to fight the menacing foe in front of them, and that enemy is best called the self-nature. Many leaders are in the tent today having meetings with their captains wanting to see a great revival, but no one is really stepping out. There is more planning going into the next vacation than in a battle plan. They preach the circuit calling upon others to fight, but they go to Israel and walk about the land to ponder on the wonders of God, however, no victory over the flesh nature results and the cause of the Kingdom remains ignored. There are warriors fully geared in armor along the hillside today, but they are also fully fearful, because many leaders have set their armor aside. Where are the men of God who are willing to battle the Goliath of their own flesh nature? We have become

Is There Not A Cause?

self-centered ministers, who are focusing on the success of our own ministries, and pastors become Bible teachers in order to have their weekends off. Lord, help us, we need hearts that are fully focused on the advancement of the Kingdom of God in our lives and in every person we face! This requires the good fight of faith.

The outer shell of armor that Saul possessed never protects the unrighteous man in any way. In later years, King Ahab sought protection and disguised himself dressing as one of the other warriors, so that he would escape the prophet's words who said he would surely die (1 Kings 22:30, 34–35). His unrighteous rulership was judged and found wanting. The arrow inadvertently found him and he died according to the word of the Lord.

David's trust was not in an outer shell placed over his vulnerable body like a turtle, nor was he looking to hide among the many like King Ahab. David's protection was in his preparation. David was prepared for battle by learning to trust the Lord. David had useful armor. His protection was rooted in faith that knew God's word and His promises. David's useful armor was in knowing the Holy Spirit; he was clothed in the Spirit of God. Many are looking for protection instead of preparation. Parents are full of fret trying to protect their children; rather, teach your kids and prepare them for life.

As you envision this storyline, picture David in Saul's armor. Saul was known to be a head taller than anyone else (1 Samuel 10:23). David was just a youth. David received Saul's

Is There Not A Cause?

armor and helmet, and then placed Saul's sword on his side, attaching it to the place it belonged. Then David tried to walk; he could not function in the armor. This was not the armor to trust in; it was useless. David said, "I cannot walk with these, for I have not tested them" (1 Sam. 17:39). You can only trust in what has been tested, and you can only trust to the extent that it has been tried; only faith in the Lord Almighty has been proven true in all circumstances and situations. There is no battle too great for the one that is of faith. There is no battle too small to be ignored.

There was only one thing to do, David shed the useless and opted for the useful armor that always worked. David put his trust in the armor of God. Every believer must do the same.

Believers, it is time to start walking in the armor that is tested and proven to be true; this is "Useful Armor." David's life of faith is in alignment with Abraham; his life was faith. Abraham did not waver before the promises of God, nor did David. Any armor that is made by the hands of man, in any form, will never bring victory in the spiritual realm. David would use a sling and a stone, but his armor was his trust in the Lord. Faith equips one for the battle.

Jesus came to do battle and brought a sword. He said, "Do not think that I came to bring peace on earth. I did not come to bring peace but a sword. For I have come to 'set a man against his father, a daughter against her mother, and a daughter-in-law against her mother-in-law'; and a man's enemies will be those of his own household" (Matt. 10:34–36). He told the apostles to go forth with a sword (Luke

Is There Not A Cause?

22:36). The Book of Hebrews refers to the word of God as a sword (Heb. 4:12). Paul said that the word of God is the sword of the Spirit (Eph. 6:17). My goodness; let us ponder on all these verses and the biblical history, and let us realize the war and receive the faith that makes you ready to battle.

Saul's armor was left in the tent where it belonged, the useless with the useless. David walked out of the tent alone with a mind "set" to battle; he left the useless behind and proceeded to the battle line. Imagine right now what he must have been thinking; there was no place in all Israel that he could go; he was caught in his own declaration, "Is There Not A Cause?" His question fueled his quest for victory.

Is There Not A Cause?

Four things that positioned and prepared David:

1. David was ready and willing to leave his past comfort zone and any accomplishments. He fully surrendered to the Lord's will even though of a young age.
2. David was able to overcome familial challenges, especially with an older, overbearing brother who was filled with envy and anger. He dealt with the contempt of his brothers, that is, those closest to him.
3. David did not yield to the pressure to conform to Saul's presence or purposes.
4. David stepped in accordance with his bold statements.

Four things that you must consider to gain victory:

1. What or who makes you flinch, hesitate, or run? Why?
2. How do you act when confronted by authority? More so, how do you behave when you are given authority?
3. Do you understand your own flesh nature in contrast to the divine nature? Can you define the difference?
4. Do you know when your insecurities, inferiorities, and inadequacies are ruling you? Can you identify them? Can you identify if your decisions are based on faith?

Is There Not A Cause?

Facing Preparation
Being Battle Ready

Preparation is always necessary for anything you desire to do or must accomplish. Parents should be focused on preparing their children for life, both in this world and for the age to come. The spirit world is constantly active in the realm of preparing people to serve their agenda, and to be their ambassadors and representatives. The preparatory work of the Holy Spirit makes His people ready for the Lord's battle—between light and dark, truth and lies, and life and death. The devil and his kingdom is waging war against the Lord God, wanting to be like God. The Holy Spirit is in the process of proving that the Lord God is the living, almighty, Most High God, and there is no other. His people reflect and reveal His victorious presence. David was this sort.

David found useful armor. On the other hand, Saul's armor was made by the flesh in order to protect the flesh; it seemed valuable and useful, but it proved to be inferior when it faced the superior. Saul's armor was outer armor and it offered encouragement to the user as long as it faced something of equal or less value. From Saul's very first battle, he learned to trust in this sort of armor. When he faced the Philistines or the Amalekites in war, they were dressed for war in like manner. Saul was able to cope with his fears through conventional means and methods, but this Goliath forced his own weaknesses and feelings of inferiority to surface and overcame him. He was basically paralyzed; his fear kept him from moving forward and his pride kept him from retreating. He was a man without the faith to believe God.

A man of inward fears can stay hidden for many years and through a host of circumstances, but eventually the Lord exposes them. Saul's fear was always present, but he developed various coping mechanisms. Early in his rulership, he gathered the three-thousand soldiers to accompany him. A man of fear needs to surround himself with an entourage to embolden his feelings of weakness. When timidity rules one's spirit, then surely pride will come alongside to simulate strength. Saul was full of fears, which pride used to feign a powerful presence. When Goliath stepped out of the Philistine ranks, Saul's pride could not overcome, because his trusts were outmatched. You will rely on those things that you trust in, until you see something greater or more powerful than your reliance. Saul was stuck in the tent! He was trapped.

Saul was now faced with an armor superior to his own; therefore, he retreated and set his aside, along with his courage. Goliath's outer armor caused Saul to mistrust his own. Saul also referenced Goliath's training in warfare in an attempt to correct David, but Goliath's training actually caused Saul to realize his own lack. Goliath was trained in war since he was a youth, Saul could not find his father's donkeys. Saul was known for his stature, but Goliath's stature moved Saul to cower under the height of one greater in size than him. Saul's height was admired by his countrymen and

Is There Not A Cause?

gained him supportive votes, yet, when he saw Goliath's size he considered himself small.

Saul was like his forefathers, who spied out the land in the days of Moses; Saul existed in the shadows of this unbelief. These forefathers refused to enter the Land of Promise; they did not put their trust in the Lord's word. Therefore, they succumbed to their fears. They saw a people greater than themselves because they put their trust in themselves. Seeing the giants of the land, they cowered and murmured, thus refusing to fight under the command of the Lord. They did not want to put themselves at risk. Their faith was in their own thoughts, words, and opinions. Saul was a man of unbelief like them. His strength and power stemmed from the natural; he trusted in his armor, which made him feel ready for war. He trusted in his height, which gained the support of those around him, but it failed him when faced with someone greater. He relied on his position as king till someone defied him; he looked to his army for support, but they shied away, just like him. Saul's training in war was grossly outmatched by Goliath, and his inferiority squashed any boasts, and all prior victories were made inconsequential. Saul was overcome by his own fears; he was exposed. He was a man that surrounded himself with other people and other things so that he could make himself feel powerful, but he was a weak man. There was no faith present, just the appearance of power.

The Lord will always expose your fears, thus revealing your trusts. In times of trouble, your fears will move you to look to your trusts, thus exposing those things or people you actually do trust in, that is, what or who you look to for help and deliverance. Who or what you turn to for protection and provision are the ones you trust; thus putting your faith in the thing or the person in whom, or in which you seek for help. David put no trust in Saul's armor or in a support team of carefully selected men like Saul, nor in the size of his own body, nor in his position within the family structure, nor in his seven older brothers, nor in his own strength, nor in the army, nor in his king. David's faith looked to those memorial markers in his life where he discovered and developed a trust in God's presence and power; those experiences where the Holy Spirit enabled him to save those under his charge. Watching over those few sheep placed under his care was the very place David learned to trust God. David's protection was rooted in God by faith. David's faith in God was his armor; it was his shield against all those who would defy the Lord.

David exited the presence of Saul. He took his staff in his hand (1 Sam. 17:40). The staff that corrected the sheep and guided the flock was the first thing David put his hand on. He trusted the shepherd's staff; it would guide him into the valley to face Goliath. Walking into the valley, David then chose for himself five smooth stones from the brook and put them in his shepherd's bag, the pouch which he had with him; his sling was in his hand as well (1 Sam. 17:40). David was prepared for battle in a way that no man in his natural mind would think himself ready to face a man of war, especially one like Goliath. David's trust was not in the staff, stone, or sling, nor

Is There Not A Cause?

was it in his own strength. David looked to the Lord; this gave the staff, stone and sling power because the Lord was his trust. David already knew that the battle belonged to the Lord.

God used an ability that was forged in David while doing other things; he watched sheep for his father. God used an ability that was fostered in the seemingly unimportant, as Eliab alluded to when giving his young brother a jab to the heart. Though you or others may think you are involved in something unimportant, maybe in a job or some household chore, schoolwork, or something else, know that the Holy Spirit uses all these things to fashion His people. God was preparing David amid the seemingly trivial and unimportant. David was being prepared for the blessing. Often times when things look the most bleak, that is when you are at the brink of the Lord's blessing. For David, he merely defended the sheep from the lion and bear and most likely the wolf, but he was learning the skill that would take down a giant, save Israel, complete the cause of God, and thrust him to the forefront.

Is There Not A Cause?

USEFUL ADVANCE

*"David hastened and ran toward the army
to meet the Philistine"*

(1 Samuel 17:48)

Is There Not A Cause?

Facing Aggression
David And Goliath

The Bible says that David "drew near to the Philistine" (1 Sam. 17:40). A brother's contempt was behind him and Goliath's disdain was in front of him, yet David was looking to the Lord's favor alone. You will find yourself in such situations, but the answer is found in David's life. Why didn't David just walk away from the battle scene and go back to serving his father and shepherding his sheep? Because there was a cause! "Is there not a cause?" This was the time to engage the enemy and plunder his presence; it was not about the weapons of choice; it was faith in action. The Lord's provision and protection in time past would surely be present once again, for David was engaging one who defied God. This is the battle every believer needs to accept, face, and walk toward. Too many churches are seeking the right method and message to do ministry; they want to see victory, but they are relying on natural means. They are trying different songs for praise, conducting various meetings to discuss plans, offering programs in a host of settings to entertain and draw the people; they speak powerfully to comfort hearts, but there is no faith to simply take a stand for truth and righteousness. Ministers have learned to tap into emotional needs and cause people to connect with them. This is a useless advance. Ministers and ministries are focused on the needs of the natural at the expense of seeing them cut-to-the-heart, thus

Is There Not A Cause?

advancing the Kingdom of God as people hear the words, "Repent, for the Kingdom of God is at hand."

There is an enemy filled with disdain for God and His people; he is in the valley of death, calling out to all who sit on the edge of the high ground, saying, "I defy the armies of Israel this day; give me a man, that we may fight together" (1 Sam. 17:10). There are a host of soldiers standing around looking for direction. There are family members and friends who will look upon your faith and life with contempt. There are leaders who are paralyzed in their own issues. What shall you do? The only answer is to fight the good fight of faith and gain freedom for the people of God.

You make the decision to betray Christ or portray Christ, to defy the Spirit or to defend the Kingdom, to flee or to fight. There is one right response, which is evident in David's reply: "Is There Not A Cause?" (1 Sam. 17:29). Surely this same cause is still present and calling out to the people of God. You are to advance the cause of Christ, and that advance always begins in your own life.

Is There Not A Cause?

Facing Inadequacy
David And Goliath

David was prepared for battle even before he grabbed ahold of his shepherd's staff, five smooth stones, and his sling; he set out to engage the task at hand—to slay the giant that scourged God's people. David was ready to defeat the one who defied the Lord of all glory. This Goliath exhaled threats and intimidation with the very breath and strength the Lord gave to him. Now it was time for the Holy Spirit to require their return. David was ready to meet this opposer and naysayer head-to-head and face-to-face. Intimidation is a common and very effective tool of the enemy, it gains its power through the fears housed in man's sinful nature. Inadequacy and inferiority are elements of man's fearful soul. David, however, was not intimidated by Goliath in any measure; as a man of faith his courage was genuine and true.

David passed through the rank of soldiers in battle array and then walked before their sight; he made his way down the hillside slope. Every eye was fixed on his descent. Imagine the thoughts that saturated every weak mind. Certainly his older brother, who offered reproach earlier, did not step in to confront David now, nor did he offer to go with him. Maybe Eliab looked for David's demise, thereby opening a way for him to be the anointed king. But either way, David went alone into the Valley of Elah; yet, he was not alone. The Holy Spirit was ever present, ensuring victory with every step that David

Is There Not A Cause?

took toward Goliath. The battle scene was unfolding and the heavens were attentive; devils watched and waited to see another victory, but David knew the battle was the Lord's and victory was already in his hand.

Every heavenly battle begins with someone willing to step forward, directly toward the enemy. A person of faith willingly steps where fear could easily reign. Faith is not the absence of fear; rather, it is placing trust in the one who oversees all things, the Lord. With a mere staff and sling in hand, David took the first step toward the enemy; as he moved forward, Goliath's true size became more real.

All his life, Goliath would have received whatever he wanted, needed, or demanded; like a top athlete in a dictatorial regime. All his life, he would have been revered, awed, and given place among men. Goliath would have been the center of all attention, regarded wherever he went. He was the Philistine champion of war (1 Sam. 17:4). Standing about nine and one-half feet tall, he wore a bronze helmet and an armor that weighed about one-hundred twenty-five pounds; it was an impenetrable coat protecting him from another's assault. Goliath carried a bronze javelin between his shoulders and bronze shields on his legs; he was a walking fortress of strength (1 Sam. 17:6). He also carried a sword and a spear for his attack. The staff of the spear was like a weaver's beam and the spearhead was made of iron which weighed fifteen pounds. The mere sight of him made men dreadfully afraid (1 Sam. 17:11, 24). All his life, Goliath caused fear in others and received respect. He was a walking armory of terror.

Is There Not A Cause?

Yet David was not afraid, he moved toward the giant warrior with faith in his heart. David was a man of courage; it was not self-willed confidence thrusting him forward, as many would call strength. Rather, David was calm and confident, knowing the battle was in the hand of the Lord.

This is one of the hardest things to learn, to simply trust in the Lord without fret or agitation that swells in the heart. David's soul was vexed, but free of anxiety. There was no quivering in his voice, no shortness of breath, nor was there a quaking in his heart toward the presence of a man, even one like Goliath. David was not intimidated by Goliath's words or his armor, not by his training, nor by his advance. David was in the valley ready to battle. David was there for one purpose and one objective, to put an end to the forty-day taunt that came forth from this overbearing presence of evil.

David was not casual in his approach, nor was he careless or cavalier; rather, he was purposed. David did not approach Goliath by trying to steer clear from Goliath's stare or spear. David did not dodge side-to-side as the movies often envision him as they cast their natural ways upon this man of faith. David's resolve was evident; he was moved to go where no man was willing to go. People of faith have always done so.

The man who bore Goliath's shield went in front of Goliath, but David's eye was on the prize. Goliath then looked about and he only saw David; he saw a youth, ruddy in appearance, and good-looking. Goliath disdained him (1 Sam. 17:42). The Bible specifically records David's description in order to make this distinction.

Is There Not A Cause?

When the prophet Samuel anointed David to be the king of Israel, Scripture described him as one with bright eyes, good-looking, and ruddy (1 Sam. 16:12). In other words, David had absolutely no appearance that would lead one to think he was a warrior, just as they all thought he could never be the Lord's choice to be king. David had no battle scars and obviously no experience, since he was just a youth; and his good-looking appearance displayed innocence. He was ruddy, that is, there was a reddish look about him. There was nothing dark or sinister in his look; there was nothing about him that would move anyone to think there was anything battle worthy about him. In presence, he was not intimidating in any way, fashion or form. David's appearance and youthfulness did not impress anyone, especially Goliath.

The giant-sized Philistine warrior was in full battle array, and laden down with various weaponry. He expected the very best champion of Israel's army. Goliath looked about the field and his eyes fixed on David, the only one present to face him. Goliath's disdain surfaced.

The first words out of his mouth came forth: "Am I a dog, that you come to me with sticks?" (1 Sam. 17:43). Goliath's adversarial spirit rose up within him and he could do nothing else but curse David by his gods, that being Dagon. Goliath had a deep-seated contempt for all Israel, but this young man moved him to utter disdain. In Goliath's eyes, his pride deserved and demanded much more than this worthless pup, the runt of the litter. Goliath did not see the man of God

Is There Not A Cause?

standing before him, ready and well-prepared to advance the cause of Christ.

David was not moved by Goliath's prideful presence or his pompous words. David was not quaking in fear, hearing Goliath's presumptuous threats. David was not trying to duck away or find a better way. David was not cowering away from Goliath's pretentious praise of his own gods. In David's eyes, this sealed the victory. There was no other God; surely this foe shall fall before God Almighty as Dagon fell before the Ark of the Covenant when Samuel was just a mere boy (1 Sam. 5:1–5). David gave no respect and no regard to Goliath.

Goliath fought many mighty warriors, but never one so ill equipped as David. Goliath was basically flabbergasted. The Philistine looked at David and invited him to draw near. He said, "Come to me, and I will give your flesh to the birds of the air and the beasts of the field!" (1 Sam. 17:44). David needed no invitation; he was already determined to come closer; he was the one who took the first steps. Goliath's words would come upon himself; he would be the food for beast and bird. Goliath's end came out of his own mouth.

Goliath's era of boasting and battles, of parties and praise, of revelry and reverence, was about to come to an end. He just spoke his last words on earth. Now it was David's turn to speak, and he was speaking with a tongue that was connected to the Spirit of the living God. The cause of the Kingdom of God was falling on Goliath, via a young shepherd boy.

Inadequacy never entered David's mind, nor did it hinder Goliath's resolve. However, David's confidence was in the

Is There Not A Cause?

unshakable almighty God, while Goliath's confidence was strictly in the flesh and in the natural based on his past performance and victories over other men. No one was ever able to move Goliath to fear, yet upon his defeat, the Philistines fled the scene as they watched their confidence in Goliath dissipate. They no longer possessed the same confidence because their sense of victory was in mere flesh. David would write in the Psalms, "Put them in fear, O LORD, that the nations may know themselves to be but men" (Ps. 9:20). Your trust must be in the Spirit of God where inadequacy is consumed by His strength and fears are displaced by faith.

Goliath made grand boasts before God and the armies of the Lord, both those in heaven and on earth. A man trained in the ways of warfare since he was a youth, now stood in front of a young man who believed God. David's only armor was his trust in the Lord God Almighty, the one who made heaven and earth. This is useful armor, designed for useful advance. Goliath approached David with disgust in his heart and disdain on his lips. David heard Goliath's poisonous tongue, but David's faith was larger than Goliath's threats. David's original statement was ringing in his spirit, "Is There Not A Cause?"

David responded to Goliath's advance with his own words saying, "This day the Lord will deliver you into my hand, and I will strike you and take your head from you. And this day I will give the carcasses of the camp of the Philistines to the birds of the air and the wild beasts of the earth, that all the earth may know that there is a God in Israel. Then all the assembly shall know that the Lord does not save with sword and spear; for the battle is the Lord's, and He will give you into our hands" (1 Sam. 17:46-47). The Spirit spoke finality.

David's powerful response was the Holy Spirit's answer to the taunting Philistine devils that trained Goliath all his life. David's faith delivered the message. David saw a mere man; he looked past the mighty man of war. As the Holy Spirit spoke through David, so He inspired the apostle Paul to write to the church and warn them of those who boast in the flesh. Paul said, "That you may have *an answer* for those who boast in appearance and not in heart" (2 Cor. 5:12b). In the same letter, Paul warned them of the constant danger of measuring yourselves among yourselves, that is, determining your value or importance by comparing yourself with others. He wrote, "For we dare not class ourselves or compare ourselves with those who commend themselves. But they, measuring themselves by themselves, and comparing themselves among themselves, are not wise" (2 Cor. 10:12). You must never measure the giants against yourself or others; measure them against the Lord God. You must never determine another's anointing or spirituality based on some outward presentation.

Many boast in appearance in this present day. The flesh nature surfaces and desires to glory in the presence of God. You expect to see a person in the world to boast, but it is shameful to see that fleshly boasting in the church. Hence, Paul warned of its ever-present danger. There are always those who want their credentials to prove they are ministers;

Is There Not A Cause?

those who present their educational accomplishments as badges of spirituality; those who love their labels and titles in order to gain regard; those who flatter leaders in order to advance themselves in the ministry; those who suit-up in order to display success; those who dress-down in order to display their freedom; those who make church fun and Jesus cool in order to win attendance; and those who surround themselves with others in order to hide their own insecurities and soothe their own inferiorities. Many leaders like to bring others under themselves in order to appear important. Some use kindness and gifts, some use intimidation, while others use the power of influence and name-dropping. Do not seek great things for yourself; that is the word the Lord God gave to Jeremiah's scribe, Baruch. Do not seek to be blessed, rather, seek to be a blessing.

David saw all that was transpiring from the Lord's perspective and spoke accordingly. When he faced Eliab and felt his brother's jab, David saw him rightly and moved forward advancing the cause of God. When he faced King Saul, who was much taller than himself, David spoke and acted as a man of faith. When he stood before Goliath, he advanced, knowing victory was already secured. A boastful appearance and words of power do not ensure victory. Rather, victory is for the one who steps in accordance with the purposes of God. David knew this was the Lord's battle and David was the Lord's weapon of choice.

This battle rages to this day. Goliath represents the defiant, antagonistic, and venomous aspect of the flesh nature, that is

Is There Not A Cause?

subject to the influences of devils. The flesh makes its boasts and beats its chest with aggression, seeking to be someone, desiring to be recognized, regarded, and reputed, wanting so badly to be feared and given its honor. But a man is still just a man, and there is no man who can contend with God; even devils know there is one God and they tremble (James 2:19).

The flesh of man can appear so domineering and insurmountable in this present age, but the person of faith must know there is a God to whom all answer. Every believer must arise and live as David did in that valley, ready to battle all that is contrary to God. The believer must know the devil's boast as men wage war; that devils seek to be worshipped and men want to be regarded; but all must face the Judge of the universe. Faith knows and trusts in the Lord's judgments. Goliath challenged God and said, "I defy" (1 Sam. 17:10). The Lord God had a man ready in the faith to meet that challenge. A young man who seemed most unlikely to accomplish such a feat, yet there he was in the valley moving toward the enemy.

David never left a hint of doubt; he knew he would be victorious because he knew it was the Lord's battle. David simply said, "God will give you into our hand" (1 Sam. 17:47). David knew this was a victory for God and for all Israel; this was not about gaining glory for himself or securing a position of royalty or laying hold of some gifts for himself. David was not looking to advance his ministry; this was a victory for Israel. O Lord, make every believer like David. Amen!

Is There Not A Cause?

Facing The Enemy
David And Goliath

There comes a time when your words meet the road, that is, when action becomes necessary; when your steps must be in alignment with your words of faith. Action proves genuineness. A bold statement requires a bold step!

David spoke to the Israelite army on the hillside; he then met with Saul face-to-face. Now David was in the valley facing Goliath. David was quite bold, but now Goliath stood before him. David exchanged words with him as well, speaking boldly in the Lord.

David had to step out fully believing in the Lord. This faith only comes by abandoning yourself to the Lord. David was that man whose identity was rooted in the Spirit. Trusting in the Lord means more than saying it! David's final statement to Goliath was, "The battle is the Lord's, and He will give you into our hands" (1 Sam. 17:47b). The moment for the test arrived: "Well, let's see!" Everyone waited to see what would actually happen; David already knew. God would deliver David from Goliath's grasp; even more so, Goliath would be delivered into David's grip.

Hearing David's words, Goliath did not run away nor cower. He was not accustomed to hiding. He was not afraid, especially by this young, ruddy, good-looking shepherd who did not have any battle scars or battle gear. Goliath did what he always did in time past, he moved forward to attack, fully confident; it was time to rid himself of this pesky gnat who was flitting about his magnanimous presence.

The enemies of Christ are not going to back down just because you show up or confidently speak, even if we use the name of Jesus. Remember the sons of Sceva incident (Acts 19:13). Rebellion, defiance, insurrection, impertinence, and insolence are not going to flee just because you do not want them around or because you told them to go away. The flesh nature must be cut-off and given no place in your heart. Devils are not afraid of your biblical knowledge or your assertive speech; they could care less about your ministerial credentials or titles. Your prayers do not cause them fret if those prayers are not founded and grounded in obedience to the faith. You will never coax devils or the flesh nature into giving up or turning away. Pride and arrogance do not yield to weakness; they only understand power. Compromise and toleration only give them the upper hand. Goliath was never going to turn away nor be won over. There is only one answer and David was the solution. Face the enemy! Face the weaknesses of your own heart and win freedom. Genuine faith overcomes and enemies are vanquished.

David saw that Goliath arose and stepped toward him; David responded in like manner. He did not side-step, nor did he use camouflage to make his approach seem more inconspicuous and he certainly did not back-up in order to reassess his situation, or readjust his mindset or to gain a better position. Often times, movies about David make him appear this way; they cannot imagine David simply running

Is There Not A Cause?

headlong toward Goliath. Movies add their own flavor to the events and paint David employing some sort of caution. They want to see David side-step and employ various battle maneuvers to gain the upper hand, like a rabbit with quickness. The History Channel or Discovery Channel will make him look like he has the advantage over Goliath because he is young, nimble, and unencumbered with battle gear. They refuse to see David's simple trust in the Lord.

David believed God and faith was his battle gear, as proven in the shepherd's field. David had useful armor; whereas Goliath's armor was of this world and was no match for David's trust. David had useful authority; while Goliath was inspired by Dagon, a mere demon that pranced about these foolish Philistines who gave him praise and presence.

Like David, every person who aligns himself with God's battle plan must eventually step out and engage in battle. The battle must first be embraced, knowing it is real and that you are in that battle. Second, you must engage the enemy; the battle is not for spectators; it requires involvement. The battle always begins in your own heart before you can be effective beyond the four walls of your own soul. Then, you must endure to the end; fighting the good fight of faith ends when you take your last breath.

Today, however, many pastors, preachers and various ministers are simply enjoying their time teaching about the battle, but retreat when anything offensive surfaces. The apostle Paul certainly preached the word and told Timothy to preach the word, and his life demonstrated one who fought the

Is There Not A Cause?

good fight of faith. He first wrote to Timothy and encouraged him to fight the fight of faith (1 Tim. 6:12). Then in his second letter, when Paul was facing certain death at the hands of Rome, he rightly claimed that he had fought the good fight of faith (2 Tim. 4:7). The power of his command in the first letter to Timothy was found in the second letter. Paul himself was a man of war. He fought! His preaching had power because it carried the weight of one who understood battles. Paul was able to boldly encourage this younger warrior to fight because he had set the pattern. He was that pattern. He fought the beasts at Ephesus, preached to the sophisticated Athenian philosophers, confronted the Judaizers, and ministered the Gospel of salvation to every heart.

Paul battled everywhere because the battle surely is everywhere and the flesh nature is ever-present. The natural man is at war with God's character, yet sadly, the church is giving sway to the natural man's wanton, weak-willed, and wayward demands. This always empowers devils who work upon the flesh nature of man.

David would have despised much of what is going on today. We are in need of new attire and it is called "Useful Armor." We are in need of a new authority and it is called, "Useful Authority." We are in need of a new advance and it is called, "Useful Advance." Why do I say this? Because I know there is a cause. David ran toward the enemy. He sought to do battle; he was on the offense and so am I, therefore, I am calling for you to walk toward the enemy of sloth and indulgence; to run against fear and fret that is robbing faith; to

Is There Not A Cause?

go after the anxieties that are stealing away courage. To speak the truth in love thus offending lies, deception, and the various delusions residing in the minds of men; to be willing to wage war, and be the one to go into the valley and run toward the Philistine army and even their Goliath. Will this be deemed offensive by some? Absolutely! Especially by those whom you call your "unsaved loved ones." You will see the weaknesses in the church arise all around you as you endeavor to see the power of Christ prevail. The devils that have been hiding behind their concept of kindness will show their ugly head. The demons that have been ducking behind toleration, compromise, and accommodation will be screaming for fairness and love. Those who are emotionally driven and want to be accepted and understood will be reeling back, wanting to be comforted in their offense. Sadly, many pastors and ministers will do exactly that, thus giving greater regard to the natural man, often times not even knowing the difference. Their brand of love is to be polite, nice, and accepting of everyone and everything in order to prove that they are righteous people. Why? Because they lack true righteousness, which is the Lord our righteousness. They are very much in the natural themselves and do not want to change. They have acquired a fancy for their own version of spirituality, and love the attention it awards them.

Beware of all such men and women of God who call for compromise and promote a loving touch at the expense of holiness. No man or woman of God will cater to the natural man; they see it as David saw Goliath. You are called to be

Is There Not A Cause?

holy as God is holy. This does not mean one is to be caustic in order to show that he is holy; that is foolishness. No one is to be harsh just for the sake of being harsh; this is often times an insecure person trying to be holy and has not completely surrendered to the love of God, which delivers you from fear. The fruit of the Spirit produces such qualities and this fruit is of the Spirit.

There is, however, the natural man's attempt to produce its own version of that fruit and call it spiritual. The believer who has the Useful Anointing, Useful Authority, and Useful Armor will promote and seek to preserve the fruit of the Spirit, not a counterfeit version of it. There is nothing more dangerous in the Church than the natural man walking about with his own version of spirituality, and there is nothing more idiotic than the man of God accepting it. Why placate and please man in order to be liked, loved and followed? This is foolishness and it undermines your relationship with God.

As Paul said to Timothy: "But evil men and impostors will grow worse and worse, deceiving and being deceived" (2 Tim. 3:13). IS THERE NOT A CAUSE? Surely there is a cause; just look around with the eyes of the Spirit!

Is There Not A Cause?

Facing The Unrighteous
David And Goliath

David was prepared and tested in obscurity and then revealed in the public eye battling Goliath. The Lord uncloaked David's faith and revealed him to the eyes of all man; this was God's man. The David and Goliath story also revealed the Flesh life versus the Faith life. Sunday school stories have fallen short by teaching the storyline of David and Goliath, but not the faith of David. Children grow up knowing about David, but never learning how to fight like David. Faith to fight can be learned by the youngest child. Sadly, many teaching the biblical stories think that children are too young to understand; these teachers are seeing with natural eyes. Once a child has the Spirit of God, he or she will be able to learn, understand, and apply faith to fight and overcome fear, timidity, insecurities, and the weaknesses of the flesh. A child can live an overcomer's life.

Also, you must approach the battle as David demonstrated. He did not waver, duck, or navigate his way to protect himself. He moved head-long, hurried forward and directly toward the enemy (1 Sam. 17:48). David welcomed the fight because he saw victory even before the first step took place. David did not wait to hear from God before he spoke and before each step, rather, he knew God. David knew what to say and what to do because the Spirit was upon him. In like manner the Spirit is in you. You can declare and demonstrate

Is There Not A Cause?

a righteous life with full confidence. A champion for Christ will know Him and know the good fight of faith.

So many approach life with hesitation and apprehension, always wanting to "make sure" they did things right by first checking. They fear correction. Pride is present and keeping them in a state of making sure before they speak or step.

So many others manipulate and maneuver to get ahead, in order to gain the upper hand, and to advance themselves in some way, especially in position and for pay. They want to prosper; they long for acknowledgement, seeking to get titles and certificates of accomplishment or achievement. They desire approval and prove themselves superior in some way. All these quests are of the natural man who wants to get-ahead in this life. This is very present in today's ministry; it is a lack of trust in the Almighty God who gives the increase.

Paul moved onward and upward to the higher calling in Christ Jesus and considered all accomplishments in this life as dung. Paul's pedigree according to the natural was useless, unless it was able to aid him in presenting Christ and promoting the Kingdom of God. Recently, a Bible College asked their professors to provide a photo that would display some insight into the teacher's life; one teacher's photo was a Harley leather jacket, another was a funny face, and another stood in front of his educational degrees and ministerial certificates on his office wall. This is not the spirituality that advances the cause of the Kingdom. Is there not a cause? This cause is in your everyday life. There are battles being waged, both great and small, but equally important.

Is There Not A Cause?

Just recently my son Adam, a mortgage broker, was involved with a business deal that fell apart. An older woman and her husband, who is incapacitated with cancer, had put a $15,000.00 down-payment on a home. The sale fell apart because of some financial documents and other issues. Therefore, Adam lost the sale. However, the seller decided to keep the deposit. Calls were made, but the seller would not return the money. The realtor, though a Christian, walked away from the woman and so did her attorney. The woman had enough to bear, already contending with her husband's illness; therefore, she stopped waiting for the money's return. However, Adam kept pursuing, calling, and stating the woman's case. He fought for her, though there was nothing in it for him. After three months, the woman received her deposit. Adam fought for what was right, not to get something for himself. Was there not a cause? Fifteen thousand dollars was needed by this woman. Many want to be known for fighting the big battles, but this was this woman's big battle, and a champion arrived to fight for her.

In another case, Laura, a young mother of four in our church, watched a sixteen year old boy walk into their yard, grab her children's pumpkins and smash them in the street. The next day she saw this young man working on his car across the street, diagonally from her home. She called for her kids, grabbed their hands, and walked across the street to confront him. Arriving, the young man turned and looked at her; she said, "Young man, you smashed my kid's pumpkins. You owe them an apology." He put his head down slightly

Is There Not A Cause?

and said, "Yes, sorry kids." Then Laura said, "Young man, there's more to life than smashing pumpkins." Why would she put herself through all this hassle? Why not just let it go and buy four more pumpkins? Why not just tell the kids that the young man is rude and ruined and walk away? Because, "Is There Not A Cause?"

My son's family moved into a home near the local high school. His wife Katie and her small children were all playing outside in the afternoon when school was let out. As the big kids walked by their home the foul language was evident. After a few days of thinking and praying, Katie met them outside with a command; she stopped them in the street, pointed to two points in the street and told them, "Between that point and this point, the language stops. Yes?" From that point onward the language did stop. More so, they started greeting her and her children. "Hi Mrs. Cote!" "Hi kids!" Why not just bring her kids inside the house during that certain time frame? Why not tell her kids to ignore it or tell them that they have to get used to it because that's how everyone talks in school?" Because, "Is There Not A Cause?"

In our church, Jennifer, a woman with six children and much to do, saw the local school offering various after-school programs that helped no one develop skills for life and living. She decided to address the school and ask them if she could offer a Bible class. After a bit of haggling and explaining, it was approved. She now goes to that school every week and has children hearing faith, and those kids see it in her life. This has not been a hassle-free endeavor; the main problem

Is There Not A Cause?

has been with parents. Many of them loved the idea until their own lack was exposed. Then it became a war. Yet, Jennifer goes every week and ministers to those kids who arrive with expectant hearts. Why not just stay home? Why put up with the time-consuming task? Because! Is There Not A Cause?

Fight that good fight of faith and own that piece of ground. Wherever you stand must become the place of the Spirit. There, bring death into subjection to life, impurity into submission to purity. Remember, darkness surrenders to light! Trust God and step out. You must put your hand on Goliath; it is not the other way around. There are too many pacifists in the church, too many pleasers, too many politicians, too many posers, too many pandering after positions and pay, too many pampering pastors looking to be liked and loved by the people. Saul's mindset wants the people's adoration as they build a look of success for others to envy. The church in these latter-days needs prophets who truly speak for God, not just mouth words and make decrees that please people and put a paycheck in the pastor's pocket. Is There Not A Cause?

Surely David's life reflects trusting God for any advancement. He did not manipulate or maneuver, or navigate to gain the anointing from Samuel over his brothers; he did not sway King Saul with persuasive words of flattery; he did not attempt to win over Goliath with compromise or concessions, and he did not try ways to intimidate Goliath or his own brothers. David simply ran toward the problem and attacked. David's faith trusted in the Living God and he was purposed in his heart possessing the desires of God; it did not

Is There Not A Cause?

matter to him what the people thought; it mattered what was in the mind of God.

Goliath was the best that the flesh had to offer, yet he was no match for the man of faith. Faith sees past the trouble or the problem; faith sees things as though there was no trouble or problem, because faith removes the trouble or problem. David could see the valley floor absent of Goliath's presence; this giant would be removed and Israel would have free reign. Faith advances toward all problems and troubles by seeing the plan and purpose of God. David's faith required the work; he set out to the task at hand, that is, to fight.

David ran toward the foul-mouthed enemy, who dared to blaspheme the Lord God Almighty. The young warrior reached into his familiar bag, which now held the five smooth stones that he carefully selected from the river bed. These would serve as his projectiles to be cast from his well-used sling. David's choice was not arbitrary; he knew what sort of stones would fly forth through the air unencumbered. The smooth stones would be truer than stones with jagged edges or a bulging surface. Smooth stones would be more apt to find their target. David took care of the little things, even though the battle belonged to the Lord. David's care to the slightest or smallest issue was not left unattended.

In the same manner that David chose stones fit for war, so David was chosen by the Lord to conduct war against the false god of the Philistines. David was the Lord's stone who was being cast toward the head of heaven's enemies. David was in the Lord's hand and comfortable to be so.

Is There Not A Cause?

David relinquished control and did not battle under the delusion that he was able to gain victory on his own. He did not see his past success as a reason to boast in his own abilities; rather, his boast was always in the Lord. David's faith submitted to the Lord and lived with the mindset that basically said, "Use me and see fit to do with me as You will O Lord God." David's life was on the line, as faith willingly does so, because it knows there is a cause worth fighting for.

The sling that served David against the lion and bear would now work to stop this giant warrior of carnality in his tracks. David's arm began its motion to attack with sling and stone. As he learned through countless times of practice and in the times that he stood between the sheep and the predator, now David's sling moved about in its circle. He then let it go at the precise time; the stone flew out of its pocket and found its place in Goliath's forehead, just under the giant's helmet (1 Sam. 17:49). The stone went deep and caused Goliath to fall to the ground with a thud. The nine and one-half foot warrior, trained from his youth, who had never fallen to any foe, now lay on the ground dead. He now resembled his master Dagon, who also once found his place on the ground without head or hands lying before the Ark of the Covenant which was placed in Dagon's temple (1 Sam. 5:2–4).

Goliath's face kissed the dirt, dust you are and dust you shall be. The stone landed squarely in his forehead; its force imbedded the stone deep. The vulnerable spot was found and Goliath's entire body went catatonic; his tongue stopped boasting; it was now cut-off from its pride. Goliath was felled

Is There Not A Cause?

by a mere stone that was cast toward him by a young man who simply believed God and took his stand against one who defied the armies of the Lord. David was God's little stone being thrust toward Dagon to crush this devil's pompous stance, thus illustrating the devil's end by the seed of David.

Spiritual entities in the heavens made their boast and would gloat in Goliath's presence before Israel. Devils like Dagon pride themselves in any victory over God Almighty, but their success is always a feigned win as God's will and ways prove supreme. Dagon's attempts to be victorious over Israel fell short and would result in David's rise to be king.

In his belief, David advanced when opposition arose and confronted him; his belief stood fast and then moved forward. Faith does not retreat from such carnal measures or fierce foes of flesh. Faith does not yield to those who walk in unbelief. Faith must realize that there is a cause worth opposing. Battles of carnality and unbelief rage all around us, but faith must be willing to speak, act, and battle for all that belongs to the Lord. Too many saints are cowering behind false ideals that seek to excuse sin, embrace wickedness, and love sinners through pleasing and appeasing, hoping to win them over. Scripture does not promote this sort of thinking. Saints must oppose carnality in its ranks; saints must be righteous and willing to face unbelief head-on. There is no good thing residing within the confines of unbelief.

Today, the enemy of faith seeks to advance its cause under the banner of a redefined love, but it is at the expense of holiness. This is not the love of the Lord. Beware of the

Is There Not A Cause?

devil's agenda and do not be ignorant of his presence. There is only one way to win and gain victory over carnality of any sort; it is by way of faith and true faith does not excuse unbelief, which is always calloused toward God and holds contempt for all that is holy and righteous.

David gained complete victory over Goliath and then David ended the story of Goliath. David struck the giant warrior using a sling and a stone, but his task was not yet completed. Earlier, David told Goliath that he would kill him and take his head and give his carcass to the birds of the air and the beasts of the field (1 Sam. 17:46). David would be true to his word, just as the Lord is true. David now stood above the one who once towered over all other men. Goliath would never rise again. David then used Goliath's own sword and decapitated him.

David had Goliath's head in his hand; in other words, victory was in his hand. The weapon that brought destruction to so many was now used on Goliath. Scripture records, "So David prevailed over the Philistine with a sling and a stone, and struck the Philistine and killed him. But there was no sword in the hand of David. Therefore David ran and stood over the Philistine, took his sword and drew it out of its sheath and killed him, and cut off his head with it. And when the Philistines saw that their champion was dead, they fled" (1 Sam. 17:50–51).

David cut off Goliath's head using Goliath's own sword. Goliath's tongue was severed. The very tongue that blasphemed the Lord, mocked His presence and people,

Is There Not A Cause?

defied His purpose, and ignored the Lord's warning, was cut-off from his body. His body was cut-off from his head; his mind was no longer planning an assault; his forty-day taunt ended. The devils were also cut-off from the one who served them. He was cut-off and his tale of defeat would be told throughout the ages. Goliath's entire life was for one actual purpose; he was raised up by God to boast and brag in a host of victories so that David's victory would be magnanimous!

The wicked arise, prosper, and seem to flourish mightily. However, their end is sure. They will surely be slaughtered in due season as an offering to the Lord (Ps. 92:7). The Bible provides ample evidence of the great slaughter that is coming to the earth and upon all the wicked. Isaiah said, "For the indignation of the LORD is against all nations, and His fury against all their armies; He has utterly destroyed them, He has given them over to the slaughter" (Isa. 34:2). The Book of Revelation gives a bit of insight to it and gives a description of this great judgment (Rev.14:14–20). Revelations also gives this dire warning: "Come out of her, my people, lest you also share in her sins, and lest you receive of her plagues" (Rev. 18:4). The admonishment is throughout Scripture.

God has amply revealed the coming judgment, as well as the offering of salvation. Yet many live as though there is no God, while others who know of Him, choose to conduct their lives as though all is well, regardless of their lifestyle before God. But David gave the answer to this foolishness when he wrote, "Why do the wicked renounce God? He has said in his heart, 'You will not require an account' " (Ps. 10:13).

Is There Not A Cause?

Solomon followed up with his insight to the issue and wrote, "Because the sentence against an evil work is not executed speedily, therefore the heart of the sons of men is fully set in them to do evil" (Eccl. 8:11).

As it will be in the end of days, so it was reflected in the Valley of Elah. The final hour had come; everything stayed the same until it changed. Goliath entered the valley with full confidence. There was no reason from his perspective that would indicate any other scenario than personal victory and glory. The Philistines boasted and blasphemed as many do today, thinking that they would surely best God and His people; but at the right time the Lord met their challenge.

Man's heart is always set to do evil, thinking the Lord suspended any judgment, but the Lord's righteous ways are always made known when He brings judgment. The Philistines hid behind Goliath and gained confidence by his size, abilities, and frequent victories. Then Goliath fell and their fears were realized; their weakness was exposed. David would one day write, "Put them in fear O Lord that the nations would know themselves to be but men" (Ps. 9:20).

The natural man is quite audacious in many ways in this current age as it has been in every age; insecurities remain hidden and the heart of inferiority can be veiled with pride, but the Lord eventually makes it all known. Then what will man do? The boasts of natural man in this world are epitomized by Goliath. He boasted and blasphemed in all his accomplishments and achievements until the day he met the man that God raised up to meet the challenge. This day always comes and there is a final day that will dawn and meet every challenge, thus revealing the Lord's answer to all evil. Goliath could boast without fear because he never faced the Lord God who puts us in our fears, revealing that we are just men. The Philistines gained courage from Goliath's presence, but the Lord revealed His own strength, both in heaven and on earth. Man's self-confidence is useless courage; self-confidence is useless confidence; it has presence and power until it is bested, then its true nature surfaces. Every person is full of fear, and every believer must fear God alone. To fear God is to give Him the greatest regard, regardless of anyone else or anything else. In order to fear God, you must first come to see your own weaknesses and faults, your own sinfulness and great need for God in your life; you must come to see your own flesh nature and its utter uselessness. One of the greatest difficulties in Christian growth is becoming intimate with your own wickedness and seeing your need.

Analyze your own life and answer these questions:

What do you hide behind?

Do you excuse or ignore your pride?

What is your covering?

Where do you go to gain courage? Many use alcohol.

Do you truly trust the Lord?

Is There Not A Cause?

There are five challenges that you must face, fight, and find freedom.

1. The challenge of being deemed insignificant. This deals with the feeling of worthlessness and it plagues confidence. The answer is to find your value in Christ. He is your new identity and your value is in the Cross. Your value is found in His love, while you were a sinner, Christ died for you. This is true and eternal value.

2. The challenge of feeling isolated and alone, cut-off from the familiar comforts of acceptance. Joseph felt this sting when his brothers betrayed him. Joseph overcame it by seeing God in it.

3. The challenge of being insulted, like Eliab to David. The Holy Spirit will arrange insults to come your way in order to test and make known your heart of humility or offense.

4. The challenge of being intimidated. Eliab addressed David in order to intimidate him, to bring him under his dominion as the eldest brother and in his mind, the one who should have been anointed. King Saul sought to intimidate David by the use of his ill-fitted armor. David did not argue or defend himself, nor did he ask permission; David simply stated the answer, the solution.

5. The challenge of needing immediate action. Many are caught in the need for immediacy. Just because someone may feel the need for an immediate response, their need must not become your urgency. You are led by the Spirit. Lazarus was dying, yet Jesus stayed where He was for a few more days, then He went forth. He was on God's timetable.

Is There Not A Cause?

Facing The Culture

David And Believers

David eventually did become king of Israel. As Israel's leader he was their shepherd. Yet, there would be numerous assaults against him, even from friends, those close to him, political counselors, and especially family members. David would experience great rejection and wrote in his psalms:

"I have become a stranger to my brothers, and an alien to my mother's children; because zeal for Your house has eaten me up" (Ps. 69:8–9).

"When my father and mother forsake me, then the Lord will take care of me" (Ps. 27:10).

"You have put away my acquaintances far from me; You have made me an abomination to them; I am shut up and I cannot get out" (Ps. 88:8).

The Lord set David apart from the common, the worldly, and the natural. Zeal for the Kingdom of God moved others to despise him; this has not changed. Amid all these issues, David continued to cry out to God and knew that the Lord of glory heard him and helped him. David's psalms are saturated with the insight he gained from the Holy Spirit as he dwelt among evil-doers. In like manner, every believer must come to embrace the truth; they are no longer of this world. You are born from above; you are seated together with Christ in heavenly places (Eph. 2:6). Therefore, you must be the catalyst who brings the character, conduct, and concerns of

Is There Not A Cause?

heaven to the valley floor. You are the light that illuminates the darkened hearts of this world. Is There Not A Cause?

As God's man David also raised up men who became mighty-men of valor and "giant-killers." Under his leadership as king and warrior, men became greater (2 Sam. 21). Worthless men became mighty warriors who won great victories. Several battled and defeated Goliath's brothers, a family of giants who had no regard for God or David. As you battle for the cause of the Kingdom, you also will experience rejection from those who are given to unbelief, but you will also witness changed lives, families will unify in Christ, and souls will gain freedom from pride, passions, and prejudices.

When faith is present there is a dividing line between those who belong to God and those who refuse Him. Friction and tension always result when unbelief is in the presence of the believing heart. Yet, faith knows how to stand fast, how to step forward, and how to speak forthrightly. Faith like David is willing to take a stand, regardless of the costs to you personally. Faith will fight for righteousness and faith leaves the results up to God. As David said, "Offer the sacrifices of righteousness and put your trust in the Lord" (Ps. 4:5). Righteousness expressed saves the oppressed.

Many seek things in this world with great commitment, refusing diversions and ignoring distractions. The believer needs to value the promises of God and seek the Kingdom with this sort of zeal. Surely the Christian must see the need to hold on to the promises of God and serve God alone.

Is There Not A Cause?

The Christian life calls believers to stand fast in the faith, to be witnesses unto Christ, and to making disciples, teaching them to obey the commands of Christ. Nothing will turn our country to rightness, except by way of the Holy Spirit, who revives hearts to righteousness. Families are in desperate need of believers who will simply rise up and take a stand for what is biblically right and good, calling all to awaken to righteousness; this is true revival. The King of kings calls, commands, and commissions His followers to, "Stand fast in the faith, be brave, be strong. Let all that you do be done in love" (1 Cor. 16:13–14).

There is a great battle in the heavens being played out in the lives of mankind. The troubles of the latter-days draw increasingly closer. Evil is being called good and good is being called evil. This is not the time to give in and tolerate such practices and warped thinking; rather, it is time to reveal that you are a true witness of the Lord, His disciple. You cannot simply yield to the culture, accept the perversion, and soothe yourself with the thought that, "It's just the way it is and there is nothing you can do about it." You can take your stand alongside the faithful, refuse the passions of your own flesh, give no regard to the devils that hound you, and overcome the world's temptations by keeping your mind on Christ, and bring every thought into the obedience of Christ (2 Cor. 10:5).

This is not about going on strike which supports insurrection. This is about taking a stand for what is right according to the character and concerns of Christ. In our

Is There Not A Cause?

nearby town, a man wanted to open a business that catered to the perverted minds of so-called adult entertainment. Several people of the town opposed its place and have thus far kept it off the map. They took a stand. But what is really needed is a removal of the filthy heart and mind who longs for this sort of demonic presence in his or her life.

What shall you do? Ask the Lord to enable you to stand fast in the faith, fixed and immovable. Then, be willing to fight the good fight of faith, wherever it may be. Usually, it will begin right in your own home or family. We need a change in the hearts of men, but it will only come by way of the Spirit, and that will happen when men and women take a stand for Christ and strongly desire a full restoration of His leadership over their families, neighborhoods, and nation. Look to clean up your home and heart, your mouth and mind.

Look to nations who do not care for Christ and ask: what does a culture look like once evil has found preferential treatment? What will a country be once evil people and evil ways have gained a certain regard and receive presence? Today, evil is gaining ground and taking over the lives of Americans in every corner and in every sphere of our land. The main culprit for its advancement rests in the American Courts, who are purposely giving regard to evil ways and evil people in order to appear as just. Yet many people love it this way. David wrote, "The wicked prowl on every side, when vileness is exalted among the sons of men" (Ps. 12:8).

Today's court system presents itself as guardians of the Constitution, yet these guardians use its tenants to loosen

Is There Not A Cause?

restraints on evil, thus freeing evil from its tether. This present-day American system has shackled justice and made toleration, partiality, and personal feelings the new principles of fairness and justice. Truth now resides in the backseat of many judges. For these sorts of judges, they see truth as that nagging presence in their backseat simply annoying them with directions. They prefer to drive their own version of truth about the streets of America.

Consider the case in New Hampshire that recently presented itself as an example. A man was arrested for repeatedly raping a five-year old and then proceeded to do so over the course of several years; he was released from justice because his personal rights were transgressed upon his arrest. The officers did not read the Miranda Rights at the right time, therefore the man's confession was disallowed and the case was thrown out of the courts. This foolish policy was used to uphold the rights of criminals and evil gained ground. Yet, many judges and lawyers defend their actions under the guise of constitutional freedom. Absurdity!

Is There Not A Cause? The local newspaper recorded, "When people who lived in the area of this crime were interviewed, 'No one wanted to speak on camera, but one mother called this decision 'horrifying.' " Exactly! The man was not found innocent or guilty because the courts made a decision based on foolhardiness. Even though the man confessed, he was simply released. This system of justice hinders officers of the law, frustrates society, but more importantly, it releases evil to accomplish its end under the

Is There Not A Cause?

protection of personal rights. Yet, no one wants to say anything. Really! Nothing?

The same mindset is present with the free-speech amendment. Once again, it is abused at every turn as evil screams for the freedom to speak, while out-yelling the voice of righteousness. Evil words promote evil ways; they preach toleration for the vile while forbidding righteousness. Sadly, the church is standing on the hillside hearing the taunts. More so, many Christians now agree with many of the present-day policies and vote contrary to righteousness. The church has grown cold toward the cause of the Kingdom, yet claims itself righteous within its own four walls. The praise, preaching, and power of the Christian are kept in the arena of the church.

Justice must prevail. King David said, "He who rules over men must be just" (2 Sam. 23:3). Certainly, there are times and cases when mercy must trump justice, according to the discretion of the judge. The spirit of the law must seek to extend mercy when it is deemed the more fair expression of righteous justice. However, today, there is an utter disregard for truth or justice. This is not mercy! This is not truth! This is not righteous! This is not just! This is evil thinking ruling in our courts and directing this country's policies to eradicate goodness from the land and undermine the Lord's grace upon this country called America.

When justice is no longer anchored in truth, then it is adrift with every wind. When justice is no longer truly just, then there will be a rise of evil in the land. New laws will also increase attempting to corner evil's affect, but they will have

Is There Not A Cause?

no true and lasting restraint. Why? Because those who are assigned to the task of fair judgment use the laws, principles, and statutes of the Constitution to promote their own form of truth. When leadership cannot be trusted, there will surely be chaos. When justice is detained, delayed, neglected, overturned, or hindered by the judges of our land and its leaders, then evil men and their wicked agenda will increase. The devilish presence of powers will become more known as each day dawns. The righteous of the land will grow more wearisome, while people of low degree will use every angle to get their demands satisfied, always at the expense of others. O Lord, help us!

USEFUL ATTITUDE

"Then all this assembly shall know that the LORD does not save with sword and spear; for the battle is the LORD's, and He will give you into our hands (1 Samuel 17:47).

Is There Not A Cause?

Being A Champion For The Cause of Christ

David And Victory

1 Samuel 17:4–11, 32

A champion went out from the camp of the Philistines, named Goliath, from Gath, whose height was six cubits and a span.

He had a bronze helmet on his head, and he was armed with a coat of mail, and the weight of the coat was five thousand shekels of bronze.

And he had bronze armor on his legs and a bronze javelin between his shoulders.

Now the staff of his spear was like a weaver's beam, and his iron spearhead weighed six hundred shekels; and a shield-bearer went before him.

Then he stood and cried out to the armies of Israel, and said to them, "Why have you come out to line up for battle? Am I not a Philistine, and you the servants of Saul? Choose a man for yourselves, and let him come down to me. If he is able to fight with me and kill me, then we will be your servants. But if I prevail against him and kill him, then you shall be our servants and serve us."

And the Philistine said, "I defy the armies of Israel this day; give me a man, that we may fight together."

When Saul and all Israel heard these words of the Philistine, they were dismayed and greatly afraid.

Then David said to Saul, "Let no man's heart fail because of him; your servant will go and fight with this Philistine."

Is There Not A Cause?

The Philistines were a tribe of people that lived near the coastline, yet alongside Israel. They relentlessly antagonized Israel all their days. The Philistines wanted Israel annihilated; they were not looking for cohabitation. The warrior named Goliath stepped forth from their tribe and defied the armies of Israel. This man was their champion. Goliath's name is now synonymous with the term giant as everyone knows. He literally stood tall like a giant. He was trained since youth for warfare. He learned how to defend himself and how to kill; he would have become proficient with various weaponries. He learned the strategies of battle and gained experience all his life. He was an impossible task for anyone to overcome; the mere size of him would send any man to flee his presence. Once he was garbed in armor, he would have been an ominous sight, a walking war machine. He was their champion, which means he won every battle and never suffered a loss. He was the best of the best. He was intimidating and carried himself with full confidence. Fear and dread fell on anyone who was under his gaze. He is the essence and picture of the destroyer.

Everyone likes champions; we give medals to champions and applaud them. Children run after champions, and young and old alike emulate and envy them. Goliath is the man all other Philistine boys would like to be; he was their champion. Everyday this champion came into the Valley of Elah, in between both armies and openly defied Israel, basically calling the out to settle who would rule over whom. Goliath was calling for Israel to send forth their champion; the one that represented them, but they had no one to send. No one was that tall, that strong, and that well-trained; they had no one to match him inch for inch, pound for pound, spear to spear; all were simply full of fear. This is the intimidating work of the devil.

The enemy of your soul wants to keep you dismayed and greatly afraid, paralyzed in your fears. Always whispering these sort of questions into your mind:

- "What will people think?"
- "What if you make a mistake?
- "How will I come across?"
- "Will I be accepted?"
- "Did they like me?"
- "What if I'm wrong?"

Always hesitating and walking in unsurety. Never stepping out in faith and trusting in the word of the Lord. Always bewildered and questioning whether you really should or should not. You know what to do, yet you leave yourself a little wiggle room just in case; you seek to give yourself a reason not to obey and believe. Perhaps you are simply afraid of openness and being vulnerable; you fear exposure of the heart. Perhaps you are too afraid of the potential fall-out that might arise. You fear what may be around the corner; you fail to trust in the one who created the corner. God is in each turn.

The first place to begin is to embrace that there is a battle and you are in it, somewhere. Next, you must be willing to engage the enemy. You are called to be overcomers and Christ has given you his victory and His very Spirit. Hence, "I

Is There Not A Cause?

can do all things through Christ you will strengthen me" (Phil. 4:13). John wrote, "Greater is he who is in me than he who is in the world" (1 John 4:4). You must live this out in each day.

The Lord raised up David who was no match for Goliath according to the flesh. Yet he was God's man. There was absolutely nothing about him that embodied a champion. There was nobody applauding him and his life did not reflect anything to do with the battlefield. But he was God's man.

David came to the battle scene and heard Goliath's voice. He heard the devil in skin defying the living God and he was irked; believers must take up the cause of Christ, like David, and ask, "Is There Not A Cause?" David was sent forth by his father Jesse to bring a few supplies to his brothers, but it was the Father in heaven that arranged for David's arrival. This was Goliath's fortieth day in the valley taunting Israel and defying them. This would be Goliath's last day. A champion for the cause of Christ arrived and now things would change.

This one day would change all other days for everyone involved and it is still true today; everything is the same till that specific day arrives. The Bible often uses the word, "suddenly," but there are always many steps that lead to the time of change. Trust and know that the Spirit is at work.

David did not go looking for a fight, the fight came to him. These same battles are waiting for you as well. You do not look for the fight; just live for Christ and be led of the Holy Spirit; the fight will find you. Being battle ready does not mean the believer looks for a fight or longs to be in the valley.

Is There Not A Cause?

A biblical man of war is not one given to arguments; he is not combative, argumentative, opinionated, or caustic. Rather, he is one who will finish the campaign of war. He wants peace, not war. He seeks to be at peace, but is ready for war. David was a man of war, as was Joshua and Caleb. War is all around us and even in your own soul; never take the position that you are unable or they are too strong; that gives the enemy too much regard and diminishes God in your life. Never think that you have too little education, credentials, or degrees. Never look at your sling and five stones as though it is not enough. Never retreat and never dismiss the enemy's strength as though it is not there. Never say the enemy is too big, like the sons of Anak who were the giants of the land. Never say that there are too many issues, variables, or problems like the days of Elisha and his servant, or Gideon against the Midianites. Never say that they are too formidable like the days of Hezekiah with Assyria. Never say that the enemy is too advanced or knowledgeable, like the days when Israel fought those who possessed weapons of iron and had horses of chariots. Never say that the enemy is too lofty as the descendants of Esau, the Edomites, who were deemed impregnable living in the mountains. Never see the enemy's might and majestic presence as insurmountable like Egypt; rather see the Lord's majesty and might.

Always look for the strategy to win, like David; even when David was squeezed to the point of doom, he looked to God and asked for a strategy. In a specific battle scene David asked the Lord for directions; the Lord said, "You shall not go

Is There Not A Cause?

up; circle around behind them, and come upon them in front of the mulberry trees. And it shall be, when you hear the sound of marching in the tops of the mulberry trees, then you shall advance quickly. For then the LORD will go out before you to strike the camp of the Philistines" (2 Sam. 5:23–24). The Lord guided David and fought for David, and He will surely guide you as well. The battle is the Lord's, be focused on His battle.

God's counsel is to bring victory. You must embrace the battle, engage the fight, and endure till the end. Victory always waits; it is experienced at the end of the battle. You can read the stories of faith and feel good about faith; the stories will inspire and stir your faith, but the faith in these stories must come out of the Bible and into your daily life.

King Saul was merely looking for a champion like Goliath; he knew that he was no match for Goliath. Like many today, you cannot fight Goliath with another Goliath. Many are stuck trying to find their champion to fight the Goliath in their life and they are looking for their own Goliath to battle for them. You cannot do so. God is not raising up Goliath, but David.

Saul's life also bears witness that he was no match for David either. The cause of Christ calls you to move forward in victory, not shy away with armor nearby, soldiers standing around you, and armies in array, but with no fight in the heart.

God has not called you to hide and point to some reason that justifies your lack of passion or faith. There is a myriad of reasons that can be employed to justify sideline living. People gave Jesus reasons as well and He addressed it forthrightly

Is There Not A Cause?

and placed great weight on following Him at all costs, regardless of the situation or issue, The Bible records:

Now it happened as they journeyed on the road, that someone said to Him, "Lord, I will follow You wherever You go." And Jesus said to him, "Foxes have holes and birds of the air have nests, but the Son of Man has nowhere to lay His head." Then He said to another, "Follow Me." But he said, "Lord, let me first go and bury my father." Jesus said to him, "Let the dead bury their own dead, but you go and preach the kingdom of God." And another also said, "Lord, I will follow You, but let me first go and bid them farewell who are at my house." But Jesus said to him, "No one, having put his hand to the plow, and looking back, is fit for the kingdom of God" (Luke 9:57–62).

This present day is one of war; a great battle began long ago in the heavens and fell to earth. You are not a bystander; you are not a spectator; you are not called to the tents; you are called and empowered to battle the giants in your life and for others. The Holy Spirit has equipped you with His presence; He was in the valley with David and He is with you as well. The battle is to overcome the world, overcome the flesh nature, and overcome the god of this age, that is, the devil. As Paul taught the church in Corinth:

For though we walk in the flesh, we do not war according to the flesh. For the weapons of our warfare are not carnal but mighty in God for pulling down strongholds, casting down arguments and every high thing that exalts itself against the knowledge of God, bringing every thought into captivity to the obedience

Is There Not A Cause?

of Christ, and being ready to punish all disobedience when your obedience is fulfilled. Do you look at things according to the outward appearance? (2 Cor. 10:3–7).

As a champion for the cause of Christ, you can overcome lust, fear, envy, jealousy, anxiety, depression, offence, hate, anger, insecurity, inadequacy, discontent, decadence, and everything else that plagues mankind. The same Holy Spirit who empowers you to overcome and gain victory through faith is the same Spirit who will move you to fight for others; because you now know His fight and His freedom. You are not delivered from entering the Valley of Elah like Israel and Saul; rather, faith walks into the valley, ready to engage in battle, and then hastens toward the enemy. You are not called to be dreadfully afraid and dismayed, bewildered or perplexed at every turn. You believe God and know that God controls every turn you face. David learned of the Lord and knew where to place his loyalty. He gained direction and strength by looking to the Lord, therefore, he continually wrote in the Psalms, "Hope in God" (Ps. 42:5, 11). David also recorded, "Blessed is that man who makes the Lord his trust" (Ps. 40:4). He wrote, "The steps of a good man are ordered by the Lord" (Ps. 37:23). Begin this day with that same mind and heart and ask as David did, "Is There Not A Cause?"

Is There Not A Cause?

Victory In Hand

David And Victory

David Prevailed! The Bible records David's victory with those two words. Goliath's voice came to an end. Goliath uttered: "Choose a man for yourselves, and let him come down to me. If he is able to fight with me and kill me, then we will be your servants. But if I prevail against him and kill him, then you shall be our servants" (1 Sa. 17:8–9). The Lord of glory sent David into the valley to meet the challenge. David had his own words for Goliath when he entered the valley; he said, "This day the LORD will deliver you into my hand, and I will strike you and take your head from you. And this day I will give the carcasses of the camp of the Philistines to the birds of the air and the wild beasts of the earth, that all the earth may know that there is a God in Israel" (1 Sam. 17:46). David then added to it, not for Goliath's benefit, but for all the saints who would hear; he said: "Then all this assembly shall know that the LORD does not save with sword and spear; for the battle is the LORD's, and He will give you into our hands" (1 Sam. 17:47). David prevailed! Victory was in David's head before it went to his hand. David had a heart for God and trusted His word, His leading, and His promise.

As David used a little stone to crush the defiant Goliath, so David was the Lord's little stone cast toward Dagon and all other false gods. The boastful became cut-off. The battle is the Lord's reveals that His battle is not flesh and blood, but

Is There Not A Cause?

spiritual, just as He exposed the gods of Egypt. Ultimately, Christ would come to destroy death and the devil (Heb. 2:14).

Everyone enjoys victory, but not everyone is hungry for victory. People do not plan or pray for failure; we are success and victory orientated. Our various sports teams display our desire to win. But there is no true win, no lasting victory, and no important success without the Lord God. Every victory outside of Christ is a delusion of success and a short-lived achievement. He is your life and your victory. Never consider God as your credit card, your checkbook, your cash account, your asset column, your vending machine, your parking meter, your psychiatrist, or your prayer pill to cope with life. The Spirit's remedy for all situations is Christ Jesus.

Natural man wants to use God and call upon Him when they need help, but every believer must oppose, withstand, and even strikeout against unbelief and carnality; that battle always begins by gaining the victory over our own head and heart. Do not let any unbelief steal away your victorious future. Unbelief allows you to stay as you are and not change. Unbelief upholds your fears and allows you to stay safe in your comfort zone. Unbelief is the root of all problems; it is the issue that led Adam and Eve to fall away. Unbelief does not honor God, nor does it bring honor to you. Unbelief only leads you to darkness and depression, sleepiness and hopelessness, immorality and indifference, deception and delusion, pride and prejudice, jealousy and envy, and everything else that destroys and results in death.

Is There Not A Cause?

However, belief leads you to hope and holiness, joy and peace, wholeness, godliness, and love. Belief is rooted in humility, grounded in truth, and flourishes into a righteous life. Belief is full of freedom and it fights for what is right. You must love the quest of believing and knowing God. There is nothing greater than being known as a "Believer." Enter the Lord's comfort zone of faith and put your trust in Him.

The David and Goliath story ended with Goliath's head hanging from David's hand. This was victory in hand. David stood before the king with the evidence of his victory in his hand. Whatever intimidates will be cut-off when you step out and win the victory. Goliath once boasted and blasphemed; now he was headless. He used to return to the accolades and applauds of the Philistine army; he used to enter his home town of Gath and receive all the pleasures of a warring champion. However, this time he met David, who gave him no respect as a mighty warrior. David disrespected him. Was this offensive and disrespectful? Yes! To the Philistines and to Goliath, and all those who loved him. David won no favor from the Philistines that day.

Your victory may be offensive to some, but it will be only those who live in unbelief; even if they call themselves Christians. Darkness thinks that light is harsh, and it is, but only to darkness. Lies and deception think that truth is harsh, and it is, but only to the liar, the deceiver, and the deceived. Death thinks that life is offensive, and it is, but only to those who love death.

Is There Not A Cause?

Goliath's head was in David's hand. He was now deaf, dumb, and unable to speak those words of defiance. When you battle your Goliath, expect the same results, because the same power that was with David is living in you.

David stood before the king with the head in his grasp, hanging helplessly. This is the one that sent chills into King Saul's soul and moved Israel to be dreadfully afraid. There was now one greater than Goliath in their midst. In like manner, you will one day stand before the King and you also must having victory in hand; no flesh will glory in God's presence (1 Cor. 1:29). No flesh will be justified in His sight (Rom. 3:20). Like David, victory is for those who are Spirit-led. Without the Holy Spirit, there is no love, no liberty, and certainly, no life. Amen!

Is There Not A Cause?

Is There Not A Cause?

Concluding Remarks

Surely, we need a faith that is willing to confront those who defy God or entertain unbelief in some way. Truly, we are in deep need of men and women of faith, who will not rely on natural means and methods. Today, there are many Christians in a variety of ministries and leadership positions who have fallen to the natural way of fending off the wolves. Too many are living under Goliath.

Certainly we are seeing the promotion of pills to cope with life's anxieties; we are definitely witnessing the rise of fun to keep Christians amused and help others escape their troubles and trials. Many are using a host of worldly endeavors to pass their time and gain some sense of relief from monotony and the mundane.

Christians are no longer looking for a time of rest, to recover from battling devils and worldly influences; rather, it is to gain solace for their carnal pleasures, in order to escape the pressures and problems of the Christian life. This is not the Lord's love, and this is not the rest that the Lord offers to His people, and it most certainly is not the battle of the Lord. The faith that David exemplified when facing Goliath is desperately needed in the today's Christianity.

Churches are trying to make everything easier for their attendees. Ministers go out of their way to arrange a comfortable setting. Every program and service is designed to

Is There Not A Cause?

accommodate everyone's fancy, always seeking to be non-offensive and attractive. To relieve any awkwardness or difficulty, the churches opt to post the Bible verses and all notes on screens. To relieve anyone's burden, the churches consider the whims and wants of the visitor as pastor and church try to build their own names.

Today's progressive church removes the stinger from the Gospel message; no one is cut to the heart and no one experiences the need to repent. Every effort is made to make everyone comfortable with church, and see the church as fun and the people as nice. The mission is in the slogan, "We're not your father's church." In so doing, they also do not teach the God of the Bible.

The quest is to remove anything uncomfortable in order to attract people to church. Seeker-sensitive has replaced the biblical message to seek the Lord. Cleaning a person's heart of sin by the blood of Jesus Christ is a forgotten message. Holy living is ignored; rather, they preach God's love that accepts them and cares for them regardless of lifestyle. Discipleship has been reduced to church attendance, tithing, and volunteerism. Children and youth are entertained by young-minded pastors who have not yet overcome their own weaknesses, so they make excuses for sinfulness and lead the youth in the same pattern. The youth pastor's underlying job description is catering to the kids. When the youth go astray in their later teens, everyone cries out to God as they boast, "We raised them in a Christian home," thus minimizing any culpability; however, they did not raise them to be a Christian.

Is There Not A Cause?

Facebook and other social enterprises are today's telling sign that reveals the Christian mindset. The Bible verse that they "Like" is right next to the book or movie that is saturated with the demonic and the sensual. The Scripture verse they post is followed with a picture, video, or game that displays their worldliness, whether in music, movie, or video game. Comingling is everywhere and the sensual is mixed with the sacred. The Christian life has been compartmentalized and anything that seems border-line is excused with the notion that God knows their heart. This is the very statement that God revealed to the prophet Samuel to anoint David, and it is now commonly used to excuse Saulish behavior. Amazing! The high-mind is deeply present in the church.

Christians often reference the armor of God, yet it is so easily set aside or forgotten as they enjoy today's amusements. Time is now spent, rather than invested; it is all about being happy and healthy, after all they say, "Church should be fun." Therefore, many are giving themselves to demonically inspired video games and movies. Many add a little alcohol to their weekend in order to enhance relaxation. They enjoy all the experiences in order to feel happy and not depressed; all is deemed good unless it is hurting someone else. Everyone is basically good, except Haman, Herod and Hitler.

This modern-day Christian thinks the armor of God is used to endure the day and help you to enjoy life, instead of doing battle for the cause of the Kingdom. The armor has become a turtle's shell from which they hide from any imminent danger. The true armor of God is never employed; it is really never

Is There Not A Cause?

needed; they really do not even understand the battle. Many today see the armor of God as a way to go about their day doing as they please; they want to be happy in heart, trusting in their armor to shop, watch TV shows and movies, play golf and paintball, ride ATVs, motorcycles and snowmobiles. Pastors and ministers go to everything secular and pride themselves in not partaking of anything worldly or wrong. They buy their Harleys and drive right past the very needs they pray and talk about on Sunday; they simply enjoy life as they declare God's love for them and how happy they are to have so many people who love them. The cruise ships are filled with Christians, but the mission trips are empty. They make jokes using biblical verses and expect you to laugh along with them because it is just a joke. If you refrain, then you are deemed a legalist and you need to loosen up. Churches are becoming more worldly each week. I have heard pastors tell an off-color joke just before they preach the word or begin the prayer meeting. They jest about perverse ways.

Today's preaching is saturated with stories about what to do and how to do it, but battling in the Lord is often far from their lives. Ministers preach bold faith and talk about the armor of God; they write about prayer-circles and prayer-walks; they encourage everyone to live for God but they lack the zeal to deny themselves, pick up their cross, and follow Christ fully and completely. Church life has become one of fun and fellowship; it is all about games and golf. Cruise lines are filled with Christians munching away at the buffet lines. Counseling sessions are teaching people how to cope instead of hope. Medication is promoted and relied on because they do not know how to rest in God, and the pastors want people to keep coming to their church. Church services have become centered on the natural life, attending to various subjects that deal with the self-life and even the sex-life, but sanctification is far from their lips because it is also far from their heart. They are more interested in the bedroom than the throne room. They are more excited about a bottle of wine than the communion cup. Donuts and coffee have become the draw, movie clips and drama programs are highlighted, and there is a pie in the face waiting for the new pastor just to make sure everyone knows he is humble and a normal fun-loving guy. Youth pastors are hired to keep the kids happy and make church fun for them, lest they get bored and look to the world; pastors offer their own version of the world by just *christianizing* everything. Here, Christ is referenced in the mouth, praised by the lips, but cut-away from the heart. There is a new definition for godly and it is according to the new standard that is established by their fun-loving peers. The youth pastor is applauded for keeping the kids in church and building an exciting program, but they have no backbone to live for God in the face of evil, which is the new four-letter word that is never used in church; it is deemed archaic, too harsh, and quite offensive.

Much ministry is highly centered on the word "offensive." Christians must realize that the Gospel message and Christ himself is offensive. We are failing to remember that David was highly offensive to all that was ungodly and unholy.

Is There Not A Cause?

Remember, dark is highly offended with light, and truth is highly offensive to lies and deception. The minister should be preaching a message and walking in a way that offends all that is contrary to Christ, even all the crass talk and coarse jokes that everyone thinks are just so cute. How many today are using replacement words instead of the real bad language? This is happening in Christian life; replacement spirituality has surfaced. We are seeing pastors preach David but think and act like Saul. Many tolerate everything and stand for nothing; while others choose certain issues to make their stand and prove they are righteous; they hope to be seen as good.

When someone is offended in some way, ministers and many ministry leaders are bending over backward to smooth things over, so fearful of losing their support or positions, or taint their future in the denomination; they greatly abhor the thought that someone may think that they are unkind, unloving, or harsh in some way. They are used to protecting their own sense of righteousness and want to be thought of as a loving Christian. In so doing, the self-nature rules the church by just crying out "foul," or "You offended me," or "You're being harsh," or "I don't deserve that," or "That's not fair." If that whine does not work, they will shift to the assault and attack with many words in order to feel better about themselves and ensure their sense of spirituality remains intact. Their pride will seek to gain support from others in order to prove themselves right; it is all so twisted.

There is a real lack in the church because the self-nature is being catered to at every level. Why is this happening and

Is There Not A Cause?

why is it so prevalent? Why are ministers allowing this? Because they love their lives; they love their Harleys and homes, they love their ministries, and they love having a following. They love their vacations and live to receive the accolades from others who see them as a blessing; those who make them feel anointed and influential. Everyone is playing to the emotions, and ministers are aiding and abetting the feelings of the natural man, who is under the death sentence of God. A pastor just pridefully told me about a pastor-friend who loves to take pictures of tattoos from his congregants and then puts them on the back wall of his church. Everyone loves it and people get new tattoos so they can be on the back-wall ministry as well.

This pastor is shaming Christ by promoting and exalting all that is contrary to holiness. The flesh that Christ crucified and cut-off from His presence is now adorning the church walls. I know of another pastor who is applauded for building a pulpit from motorcycle handlebars. People love the way he reaches out to the bikers; in actuality, the bikers of this world are not maturing beyond their biker life; it just gives a place for Christians to live out the biker mindset in church. They dress like a biker, walk and act like other bikers, and talk biker language. Yet, they feel so sanctified and Christ-loving; it is appalling. Of course, I would be deemed a Pharisee and legalist for writing this. Inwardly they transfer their own pride unto me saying, "You jeopardize souls by not meeting people where they are at;" "you hinder their salvation;" "you need to make people feel comfortable in church." Ridiculous!

Is There Not A Cause?

Today's church is basically, "Come as you are, Leave as you came." No thank you! Christ demands change! Today, we are all about sports and wearing our team shirts to church in order to identify ourselves as fans, and we call it fellowship and worship. Pastors and ministers are all about video and computer games, posting it all on Facebook as though it is a righteous thing. Others that are weak in their Christian walk view the permission slip and follow accordingly. We are about titles and positions; we are all about humor; we are all about fun. Christians are more focused on supernatural heroes from comic books than biblical heroes of the faith. Where are the men and women of faith like David? He was the hero we should be looking to. Some would now handle this offensive attack with the question: "So you're against fun and movies and no one can watch Batman?" This is exactly what I am talking about. One is ready to fight and argue for their rights for the natural, but cower in the face of holiness. They do not want anyone touching their right to do as they please. If any of them end up reading this, they will most likely see this as legalistic, harsh, and intolerant. So be it; they are merely Goliath's voice in the valley.

Ministers once gathered together and came to the great evangelist Billy Sunday because they were bothered with his message. They told Reverend Sunday that his message was ruffling feathers. They advised him to pet the cat the right way so that the cat enjoys the attention and likes the minister's touch. They wanted him to preach and help people by stroking them in such a way that makes the cat purr. Billy

Is There Not A Cause?

Sunday listened to them and then simply said to all of them, "Well, turn the cat around." Exactly!

Today's church is highly focused on praise, which involves little confrontation and requires no growth in your faith. Praise allows you to stay as you are and feel good about being saved. The Christian can walk out of the service as though he did something wonderful for God. Today's praise allows the Christian to gain a sense of release from life's struggles. God's warming presence is experienced in the emotional realm; you can feel good about life and living. However, this is not the praise that comes forth when someone wins the battle; the shout of victory that comes forth when the walls fall down, the sea split open, the enemy is crushed, or the Goliath falls before you. Victories like this are deemed passé.

Many pastors do not know how to advance the cause of Christ. They praise themselves for starting churches, yet these churches are foundationally flawed with the natural ways. Many do not understand the spirit realm and do not know how to wage war in the Spirit. People are attending churches that do not teach them to be a true disciple that abides in Christ. Christians are only trying to get through the day without being downcast or depressed. They are just "churched." They are taught the biblical stories and learn the names involved, but they do not ever experience the faith in those stories.

The church has become a culture of coping, instead of conquering. This mindset is quite far from the Holy Spirit. Many would be quite offended with these remarks, and begin to justify themselves and ignore this message. Why? They

Is There Not A Cause?

want to remain in the status quo. So many just want to be applauded for trying; their desire to be "patted on the back" trumps this admonishment or any encouragement to trust God.

Surely, the Lord is calling forth a people to believe God. Look about the land and see the devastation; decadence and defiance have infiltrated the souls of young and old. The church is quite guilty of permitting and even participating in much worldliness. Carnal Christianity and Casual Christianity are now dominating the church. Highmindedness is plaguing the church like cancer. Worldly behavior is overlooked because they look around and see others doing worse; so they say, "I'm not as bad as those over there." This is the self-righteous heart of Saul at work in today's church.

Sadly, even those of the Pentecostal denominations use the gift of tongues to deem themselves more holy than others. They think of themselves in a right relationship with God because they speak in tongues and usually praise God with more enthusiasm than others. They forget that God can make rocks cry out in praise and cause a donkey to speak when needed. Tongues is not an insurance policy that guarantees salvation, nor is tongues insulation from worldliness or from the self-serving life. Tongues is a gift for both personal and corporate edification in Christ.

The Church needs a healthy dose of holiness and a stirred faith that rises up and engages in battles, without fear of being deemed offensive. So many Christians want to prove their Christlikeness and love through politeness, but they lack

Is There Not A Cause?

power to overcome the flesh, the world, and the devil. They always fear reprisal.

The only way revival will come is when men and women of faith take a stand and rely on the Lord, willing to offend what is offensive to God's holy character. Goliath was offensive, insulting the Lord of glory. One man stood up and said, "Is There Not a Cause?" David was offensive to Eliab, yet David moved forward. David was offensive to Goliath, yet David moved forward.

This is the time to move forward. The Holy Spirit is advancing the Kingdom; it is surely coming. May you be inspired this day; let your passion be ignited. Live for God! Is There Not A Cause? Yes, There Is A Cause Worth The Fight!

I will not be afraid of ten thousands of people who have set themselves against me all around (Psalm 3:6).

Whenever I am afraid, I will trust in You...In God I have put my trust; I will not fear. What can flesh do to me?...I will render praises to You, for You have delivered my soul from death. Have You not kept my feet from falling, that I may walk before God in the light of the living? (Psalm 56).

Beware of dogs, beware of evil workers, beware of the mutilation! For we are the circumcision, who worship God in the Spirit, rejoice in Christ Jesus, and have no confidence in the flesh (Phil. 3:2–3).

Is There Not A Cause?

Books Written By Dr. Cote

The Holy Spirit and The Spirit World

The Face of Faith

Threshold of Faith
The History of God's People

Finding Freedom at the Feet of Jesus

Truth Be Known
Series One

Finding Faith in The Book of Acts—Workbook

Finding Faith in Joshua, Judges, and Ruth—
Workbook

Finding Faith in Genesis—Workbook
Adam, Noah, Abraham, Isaac, Jacob, Joseph

They'd Call Me Biased
101 Reasons Why They'd Call Me Biased

Is There Not A Cause?

To know more about Dr. Cote, or to access his Facebook page, to hear his sermons in both audio and video format, to see the other books he has written, or to subscribe to his newsletter, go to his website:

www.GaryHCote.com.

Is There Not A Cause?